Len

Art is everywhere

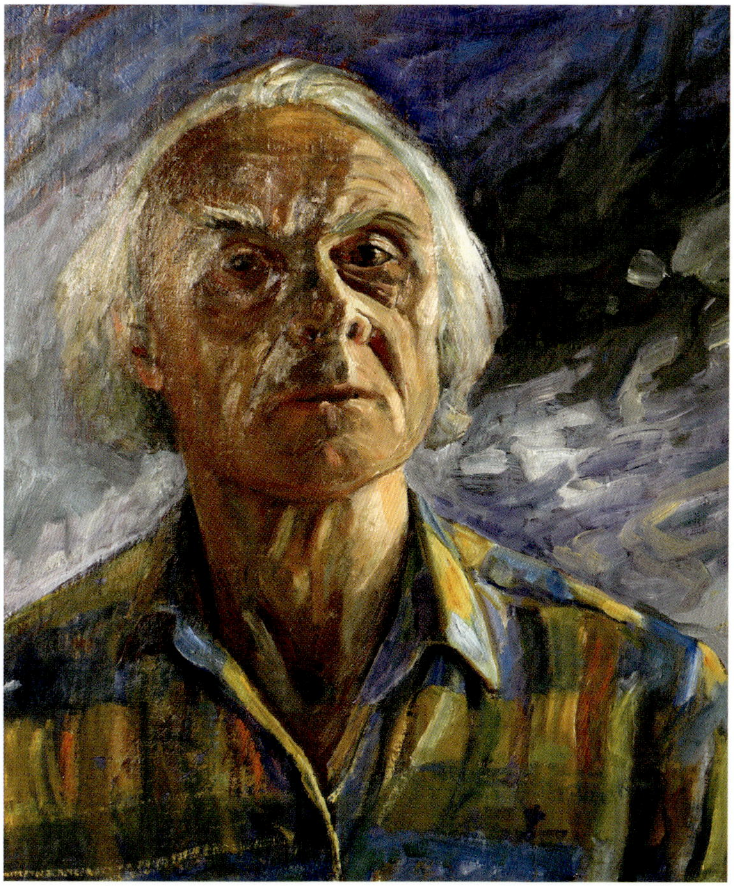

redcliffe

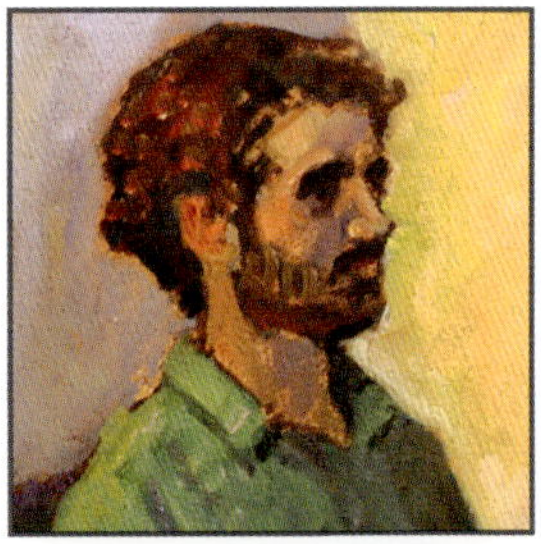
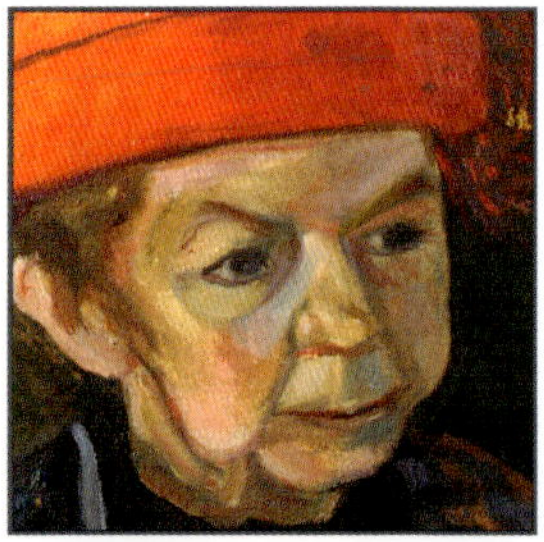
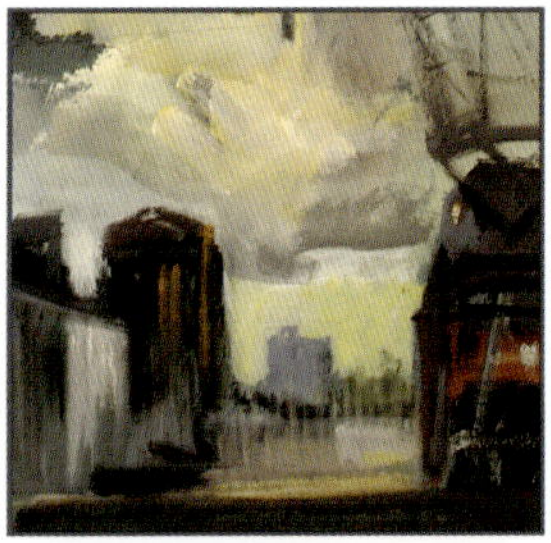
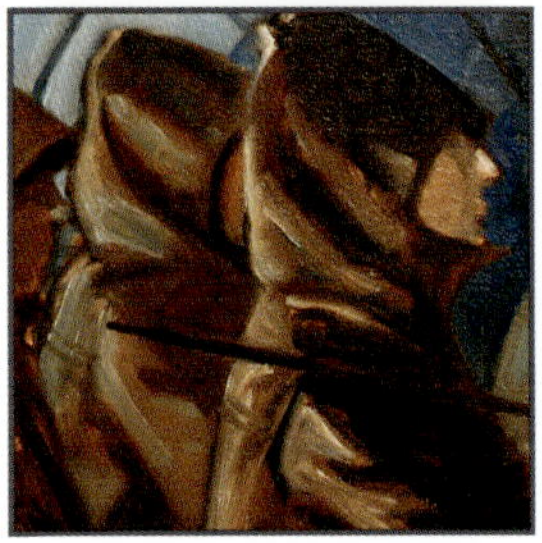
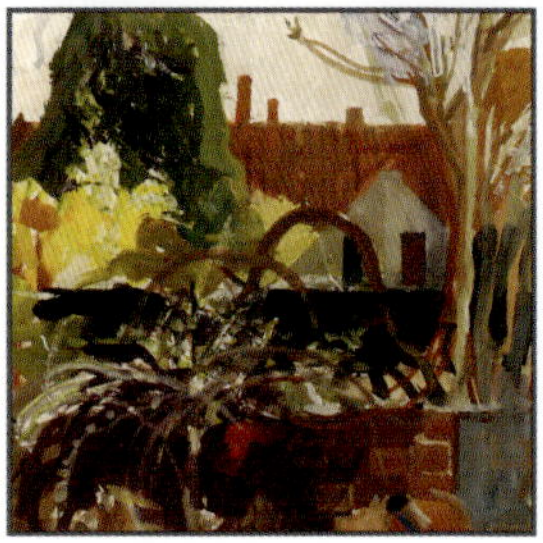
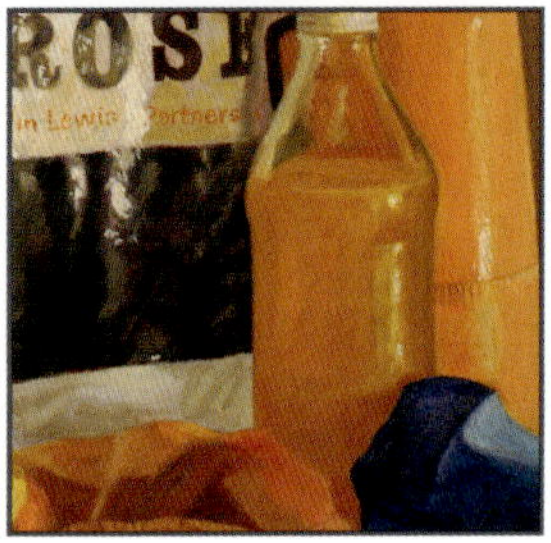

First published in 2007 by Redcliffe Press Ltd.,
81g Pembroke Road, Bristol BS8 3EA
www.redcliffepress.co.uk
info@redcliffepress.co.uk

ISBN 978 1 904537 81 6

British Library Cataloguing-in-Publication Data
A catalogue record for this book is available from the British Library

Design, photography and typesetting by Stephen Morris: www.stephen-morris.co.uk smc@freeuk.com
Printed by HSW Print, Tonypandy

Contents

Len Gifford 1919-1990 *4*

Foreword by Philip Gross *5*

Print out *6*

Reaching maturity *9*

Fashion *11*

Romance – 808.3 *13*

Wholly matrimony *14*

Case history *17*

I woke up today *18*

Our poster proclaims *21*

Sun is ... *22*

By my bean row *24*

This Monday *26*

At the word painting class *29*

How easel was chosen *31*

For us there is only the trying *33*

A formal dance *35*

Villanelle for a villainy *36*

Colours *38*

Landscape in Grisaille *41*

The poetry of inanimate objects *42*

The world of Odilon Redon *44*

Easton before the Freeway *46*

Our lodger *48*

The Index *51*

Bristoll, Citty and County *52*

After listening to Mahler's 'Titan' Symphony *55*

Liberation *57*

Time for verse *58*

Falling asleep *61*

A shift of scene *62*

November '89 *64*

Garden walls in snow *67*

A journey *68*

Christmas Day *71*

January poem *72*

Storm *74*

Anniversary of Beethoven (any musical figure) *77*

Mournful numbers *79*

Len Gifford 1919-1990

Len Gifford was born in 1919 and died in 1990. From documents, notes and letters it is clear that his ambition to be a painter was strong. At the age of nineteen years he wrote 'The practice and science of drawing by Harold Speed has had a profound influence upon me'.

Practice was important to him but interruptions came. World War II interrupted his apprenticeship to a local printing firm. However, he found work with the Admiralty in Taunton, charting shipping routes until the war ended and he could resume his apprenticeship as a graphic designer staying with the local printing firm, Mardon, Son & Hall for 43 years.

Marriage in 1953 and a small family left little time for painting for several years. He later enrolled in classes at Queen's Road. First came evening classes, tutored by Anne Hicks, then polytechnic. At the same time he joined the Clifton Arts Club. His retirement at 59 led to his most creative period, reflecting his love of painting in writing and poetry: 'the arts have given my whole life a significance and richness'.

As his wife I found it touching to read the comments of Anthony Rossiter, Peter Swan, Liz Hunter, and the messages from the many people who knew him and who found him a welcome presence and help.

Isabel Gifford

Foreword

For anyone who never had the pleasure of meeting Len Gifford, here is your chance. The poems are full of his personality: wry, modest, thoughtful, with a twinkle in the eye. They speak of his commitment to the craft of writing and of painting, and are alive with a sense that, for all his skill and his seventy years, he was only just beginning:

> *...don't give up.*
> *Think of the sheer joy when it all comes right*
> *Sometimes it all comes right.*

This book is a celebration, not just of Len Gifford but also of the world of the poetry workshop, where writers support and stimulate and tease each other's poems into life. Part of Len's creative legacy cannot be contained in these pages. It is in Polygon Poets, it was in Practising Poets – he was a member of both; it is in the poems other writers wrote that bit differently for working alongside him.

Many of Len's poems are about (though not only about) 'the long craft, the graft' of exercises, practice, trying out techniques. It would be an education just to trace the variety of verse forms road-tested in this book. That practical feeling, like a smell of paint or new-cut wood, is in the air. But when you look round the faces in his workshop circle you notice they include Auden, Dante, Mahler, Michelangelo...good craftsmen all. Len Gifford is at home among them, and he makes you feel at home there too.

Philip Gross

Print out

If I could only be
A User-friendly word-processor,
What words would come with Spring's
Cool touch!

My mind is full as an unmilked letter-box
And everything unsorted.
If Spring took me over and wrote a poem
Herself!
The mirrored sun dazzles off the road
And rain-washed pavements flash a code
To the blossoms.
There's a thrilling tingle through my
Heels and toes.
I walk on a live wire.
Someone there looks as though he's just got up.
He's drinking nectar from a coffee-cup.
Time is easy. The fat morning purrs.
Morning is a crowd of yellow balloons
Filling and filling with random rushes of air
And rising silently.
What power moves the carousel of Spring?
I hear it now like a dynamo,
Continuous as motorcars –
Quite distinct from the sudden buzzing bee.

Spring has turned me on.
My inward eye is bright as Wordsworth's was.
And here the poem comes! It's printing out!
But what's it all about?
Silly shepherds! Birds! Hey-nonny-no!
And how spring posed
For Botticelli once
In a flowery dress!

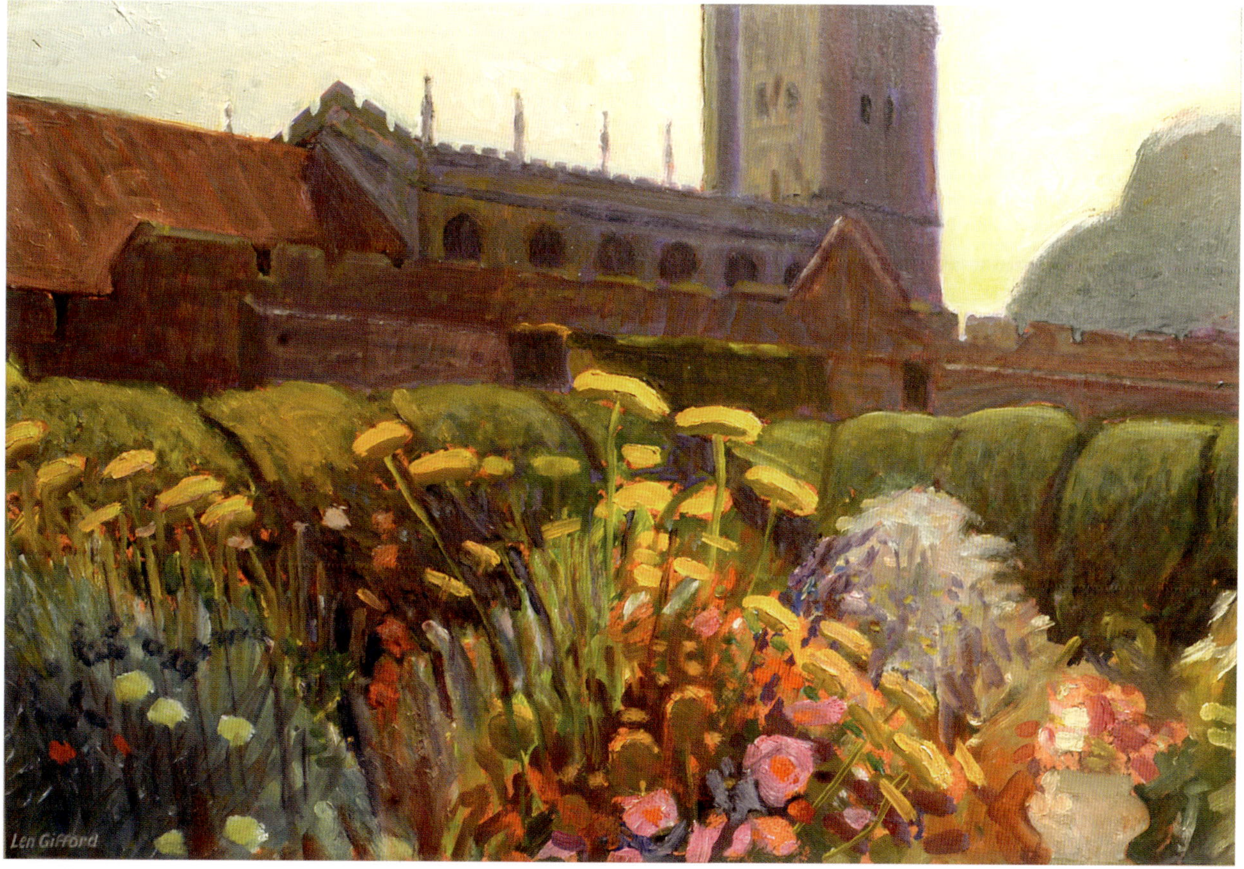
Len Gifford

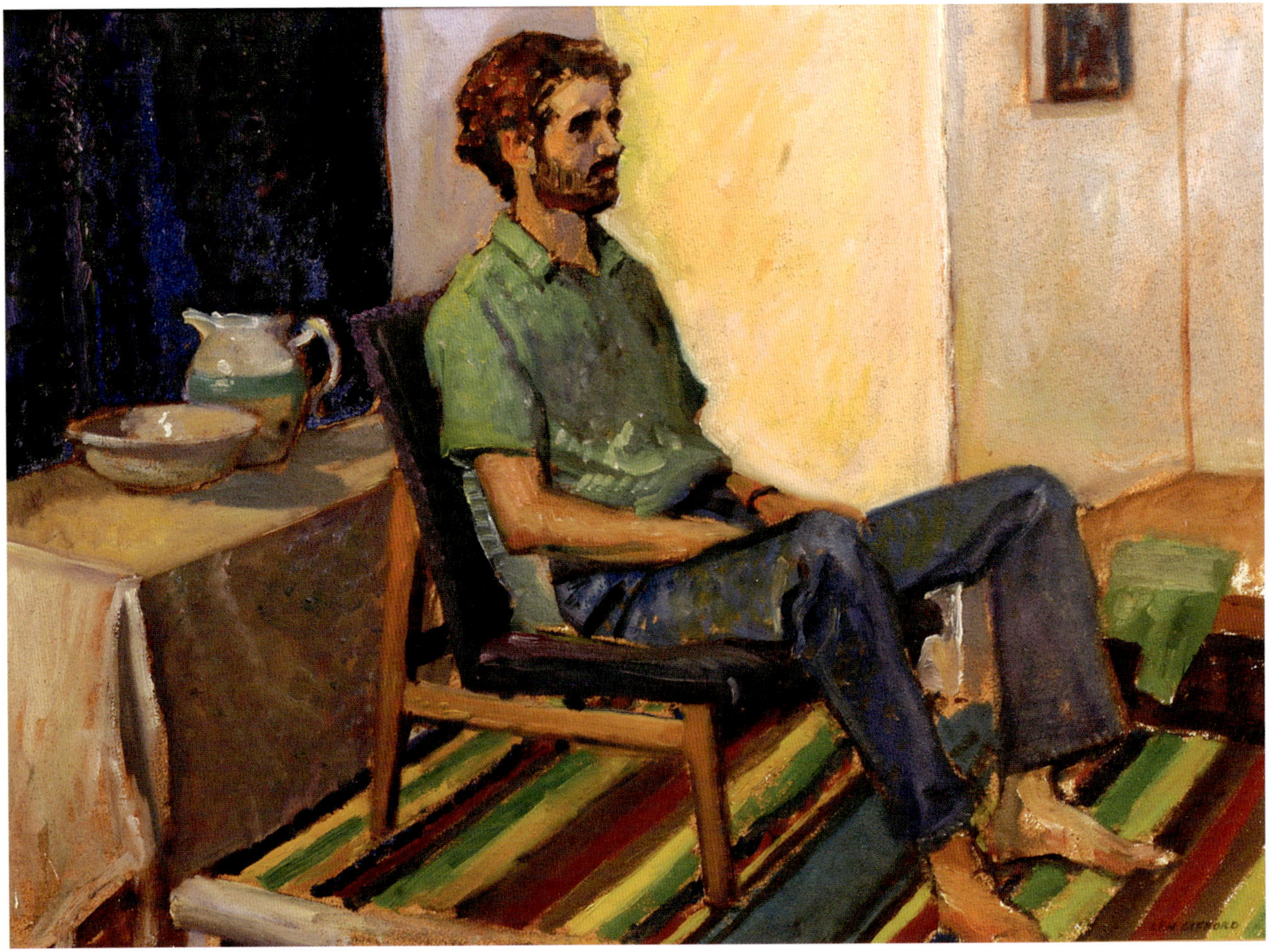

Reaching maturity

Now that my life is in its autumn stage
You'd think I'd be excused for glancing back
Nostalgically upon old triumphs – the crack
And bustle of an active middle age.
Excusable to mourn for youthful rage
Even with its fickleness. Mourning the present lack
Of dreams and schemes. Remembering even the black
Despairs that later manhood would assuage

But no! The young man's forward-looking drive
Remains the impetus of the more mature,
Still eager to succeed and work and strive
And study and endeavour and endure.
Behaving madly thus I shall stay alive
Knowing that for this ill there's but one cure.

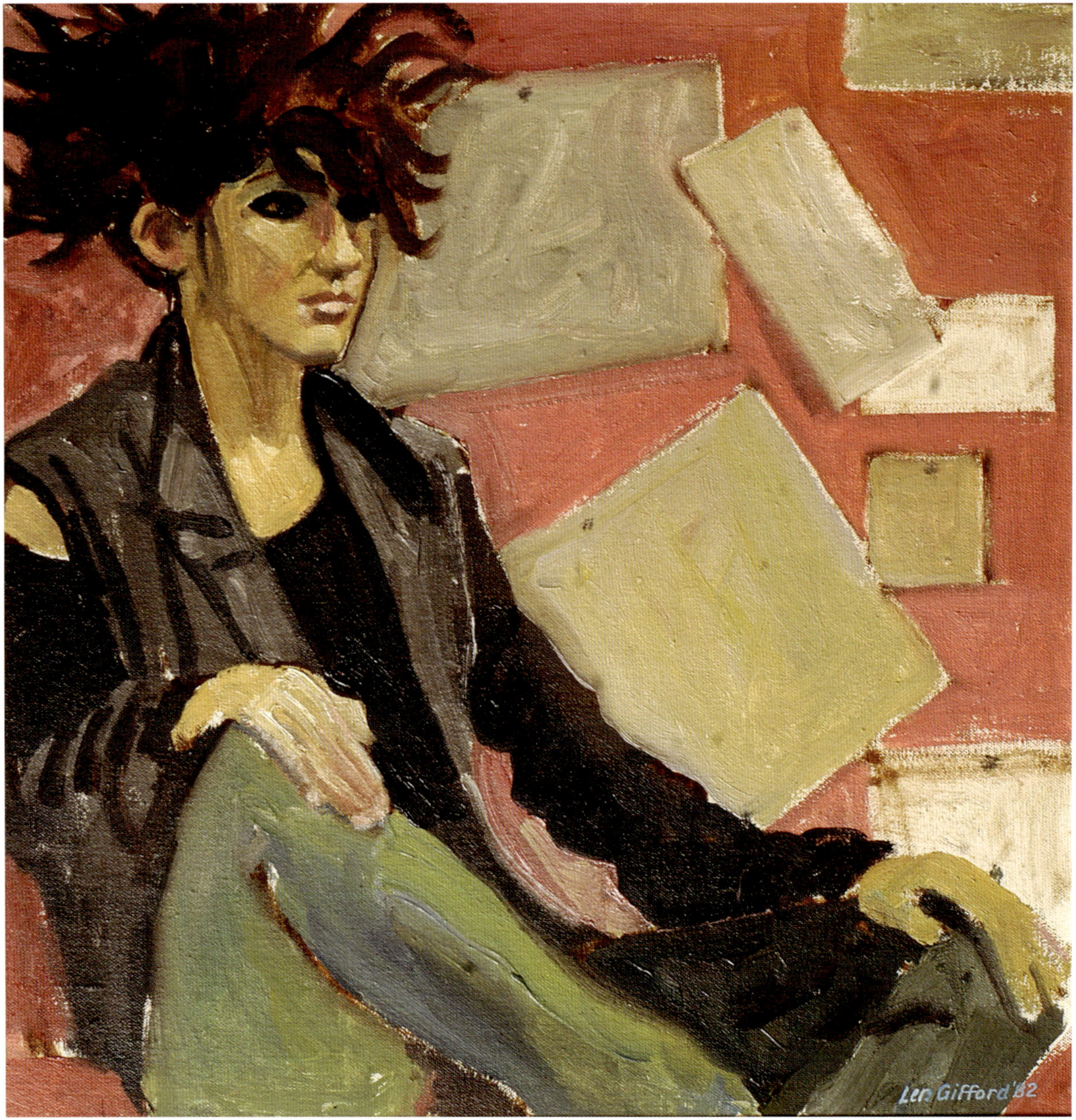
Len Gifford '82

Fashion

Adam's fig-leaf, Joseph's coat.
Maxis, minis, in-between –
Pomp and circumstance and youth
Go to make the fashion scene.

Chaucer's youth had skin-tight hose,
One leg blue and one leg scarlet
Drooping sleeves, fantastic shoes.
Quite beyond the common varlet

And the courtier, richly clad.
Wore his wealth upon his back,
Which is not the case today
Fashions now come 'Off the rack'

So the scene must always change
Now, permissive films and plays
Demonstrate the simple suits
Worn in anti-fig-leaf days!

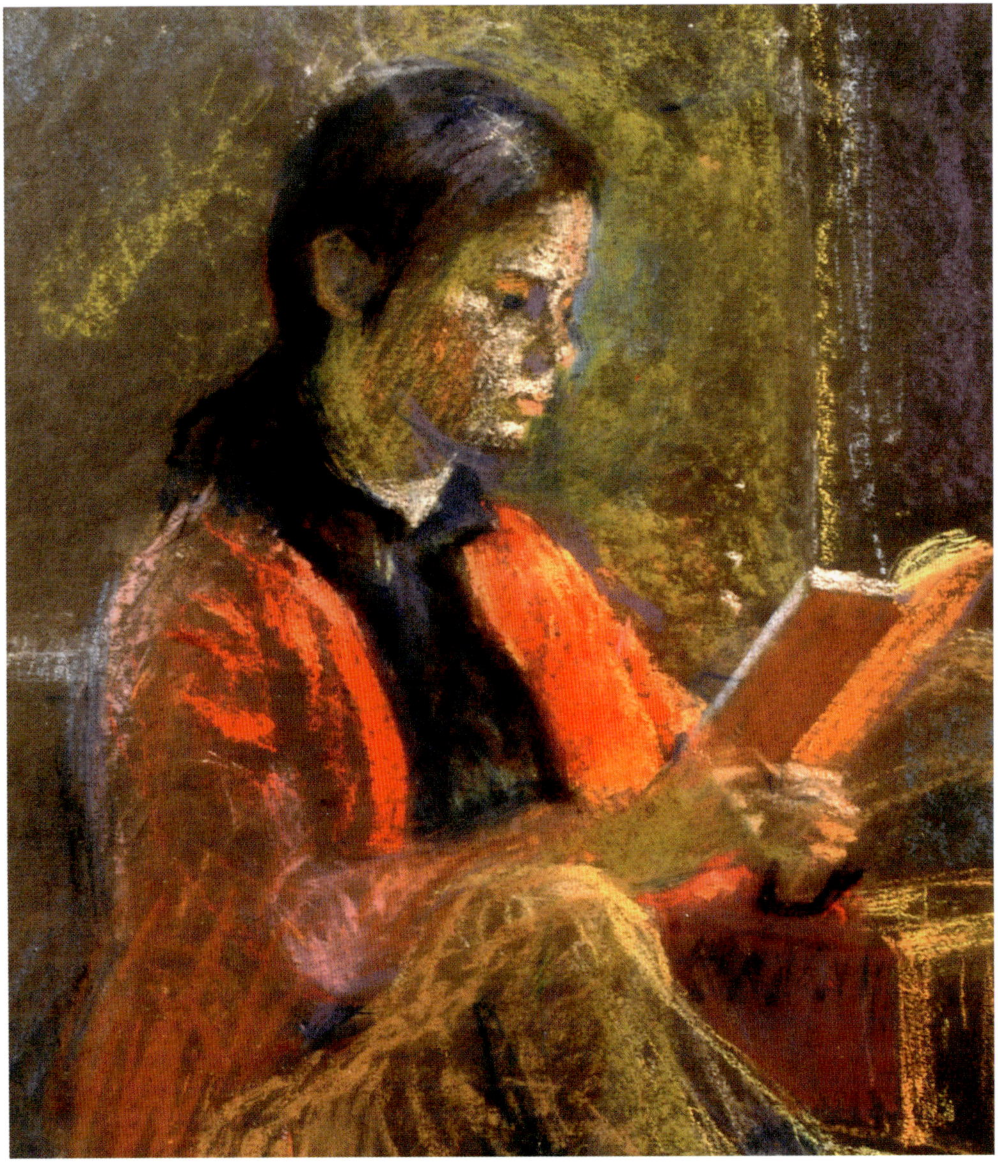

Romance – 808.3

'O damn! I kept my books too long –
I must have missed the dates.'
I glance at her, and then my tongue
goes dry, and hesitates.

O loveliest librarian!
Watching you with your trolley
reduces this vulgarian
to deepest melancholy.

You trundle books around the floor,
Fiction – or Science (Applied),
like Shorthand (653.4)
I follow, Dewey-eyed.

And where they have to go, you know,
down to the smallest decimal:
but I'm too shy to say 'Hello!'
My hope is infinitesimal.

I have no fine or special trait
for Poetry (821)
or Pottery (738.8).
Nothing to turn you on.

The library man who makes you smile,
(the pimply one) – is my pet hate:
the kind of bilious bibliophile
that I abominate.

If only I could make rapport –
If it were just ourselves!
One word from you would matter more
than those on all the shelves.

Wholly matrimony

Chance will throw us both together
like a rhyme – no better reason.
Shall we truly need each other
through the years – or for a season?
Through all fair and fouler weather
shall we love our open prison?

Walls will hardly make a prison
when we're warm in bed together
in the first romantic season
thinking only of each other,
knowing no important reason
to be careful – of the weather.

We shall joke about the weather,
not about our vows, our prison,
not until we've been together
growing wiser as we season,
growing used to one another,
and ironical – in reason.

With the open eyes of reason
we shall wonder how we weather
in the stormy world, this prison.
Shall we rock the boat together
when it's not fair-weather season:
shall we turn from one another?

Now, the women join each other –
militant till men see reason:
saying we are chained together
in a patriarchal prison.
How can modern marriage weather
such a climate, such a season? –

Saying, now's the time to season
Marriage with fair laws – no other
compromise has better reason.
This will help to change the weather,
make the world less like a prison,
All the time that we're together.

And together for a season
only, when no reason other
than rough weather wrecks the prison.

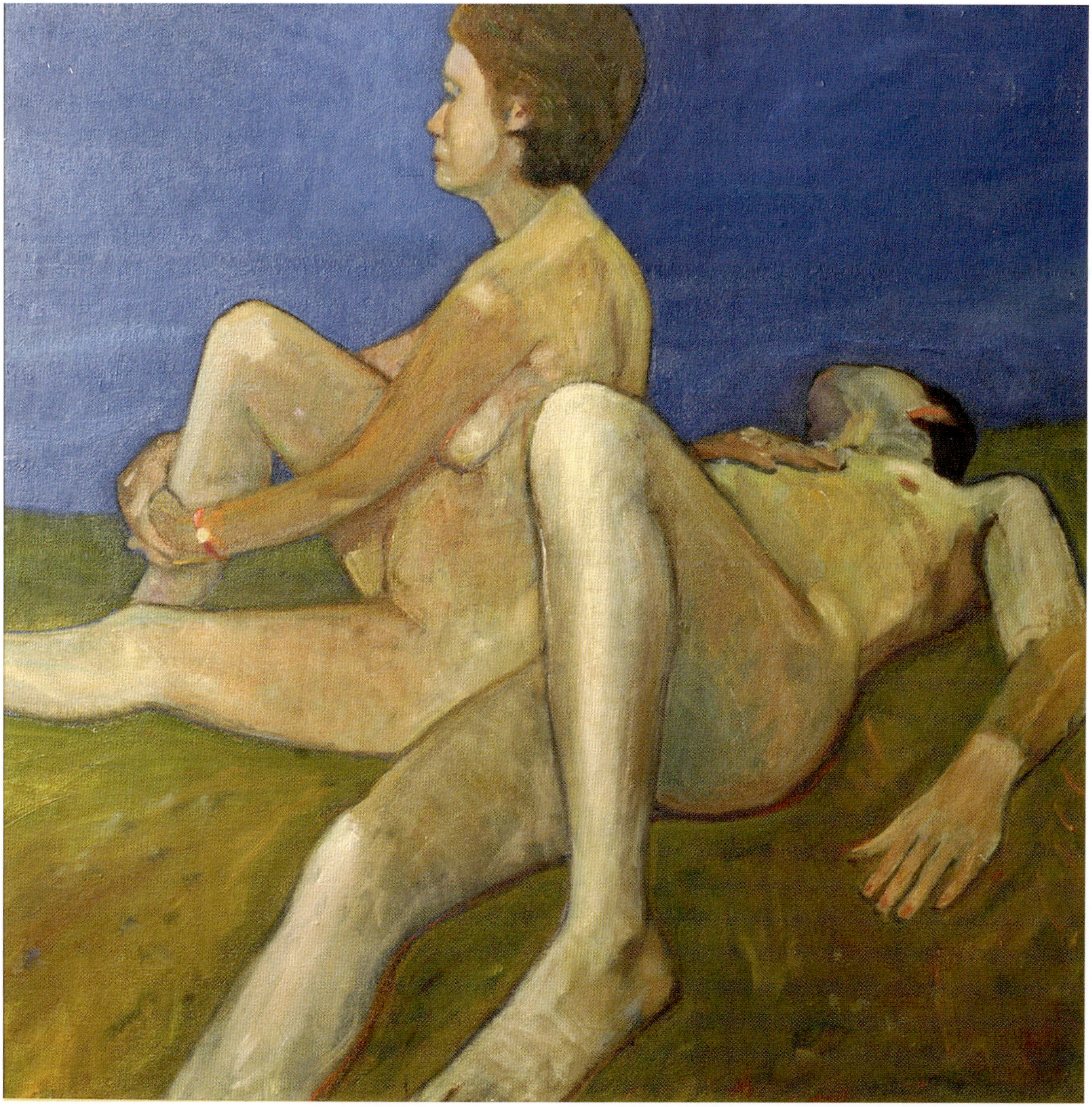

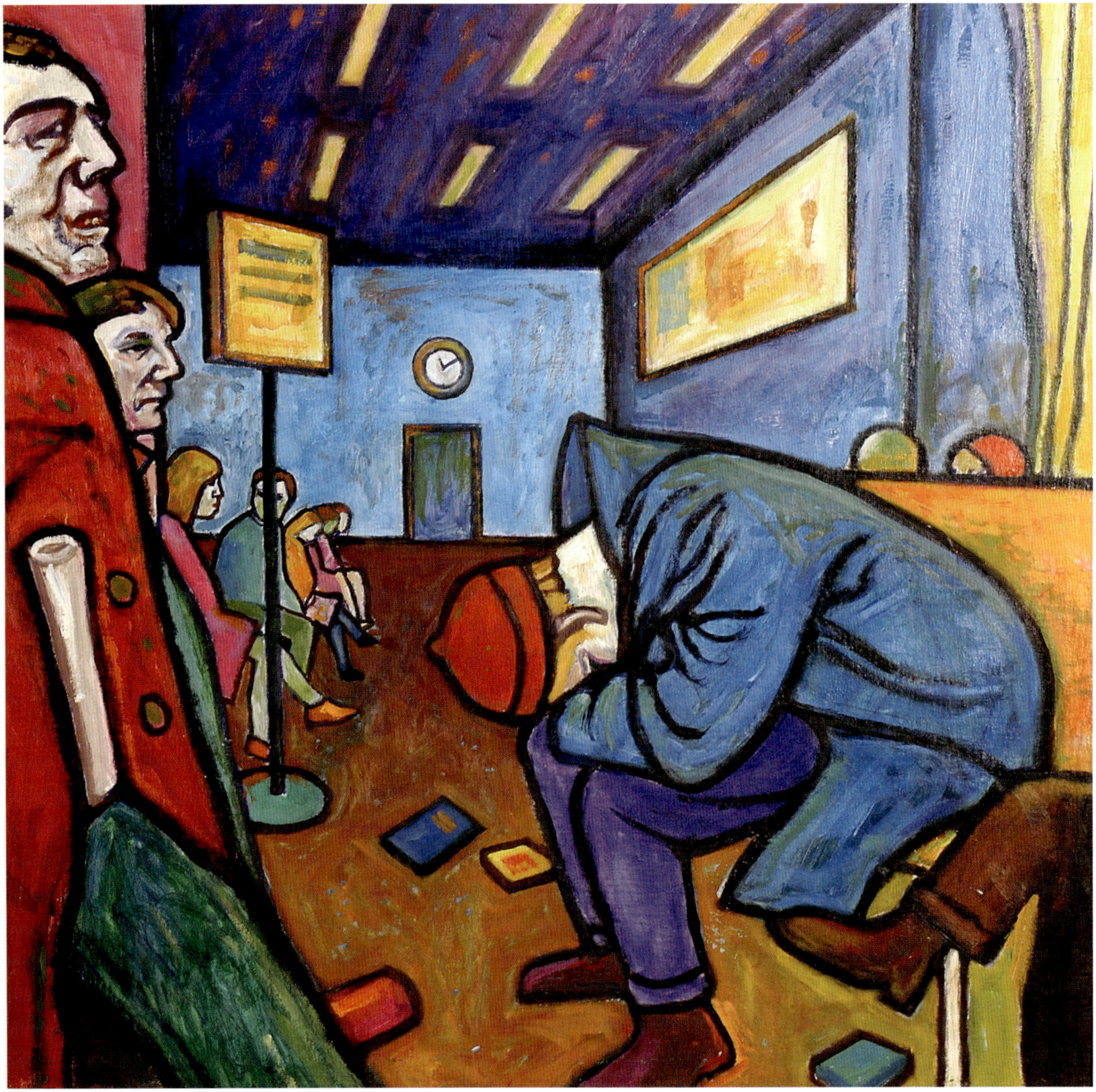

Case history

Oh Yes! We're all on social service aid.
My husband George, five boys, my daughter Grace,
My Mum, she's ninety, doddering and decayed,
And me – together in this house. The place
Gets on my nerves. There's always argument.
It's just like being in a chicken pen.
Young Trevor's always trying to invent
Some illness – and he's off from school again!
I promised his headmaster – gave my word:
And that's about as much as I can give.
The money won't go round. I can't afford
New clothes and things. It's very hard to live.
Oh, holidays? I thought I heard George say
He'd booked for Spain – Again! He'll have to pay.

I woke up today

I woke up today feeling funny
Because I had changed in the night
I have extra legs – four too many
It really did give me a fright.

Because I had changed in the night
I wondered what people would say.
It really did give me a fright
And how would I get through the day?

I wondered what people would say
To see me, a beetle, in bed.
My father would say, 'keep away'
My mother would wish I was dead.

To see me, a beetle, in bed,
So awful, forbidding and grey
My mother would wish I was dead.
My prospects would change straightaway

So awful, forbidding and grey
I had extra legs – four too many
My prospects would change, straightaway
I woke up today feeling funny.

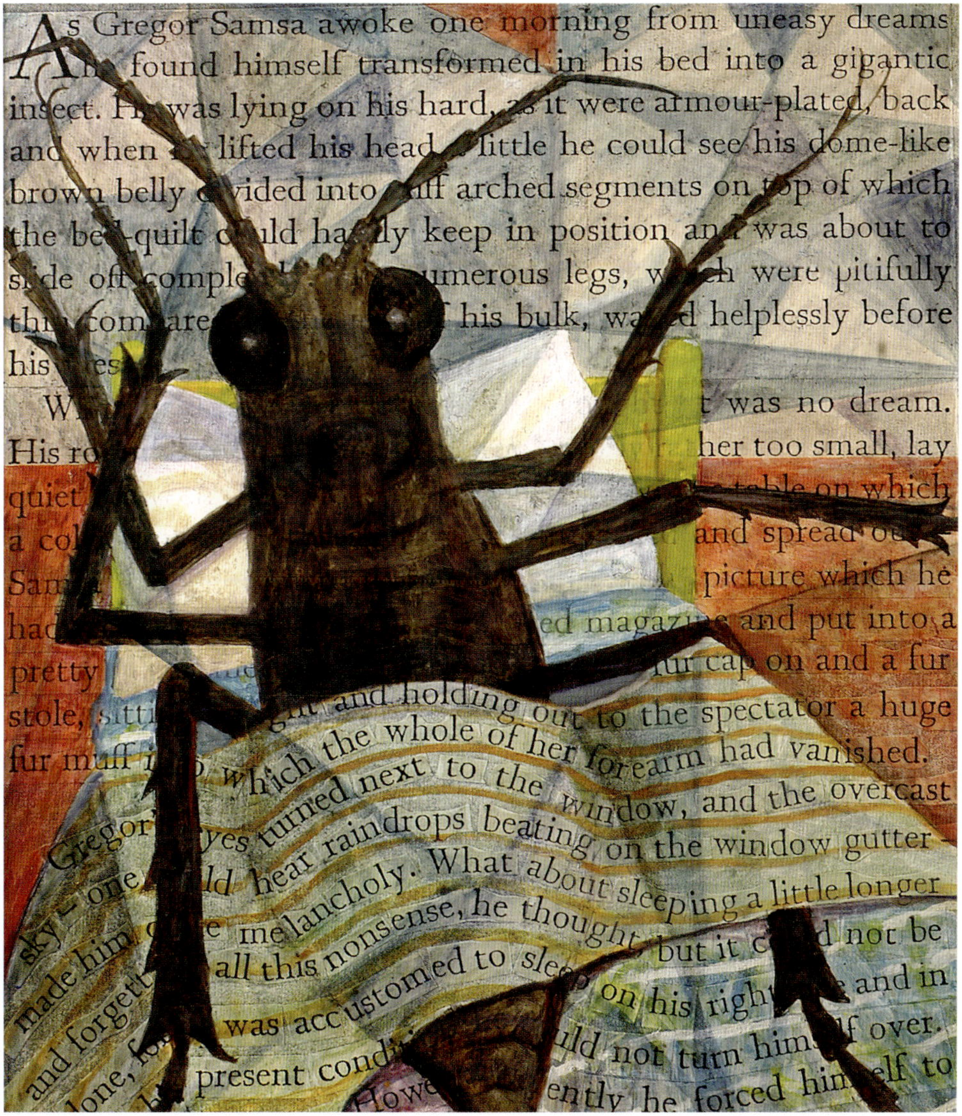

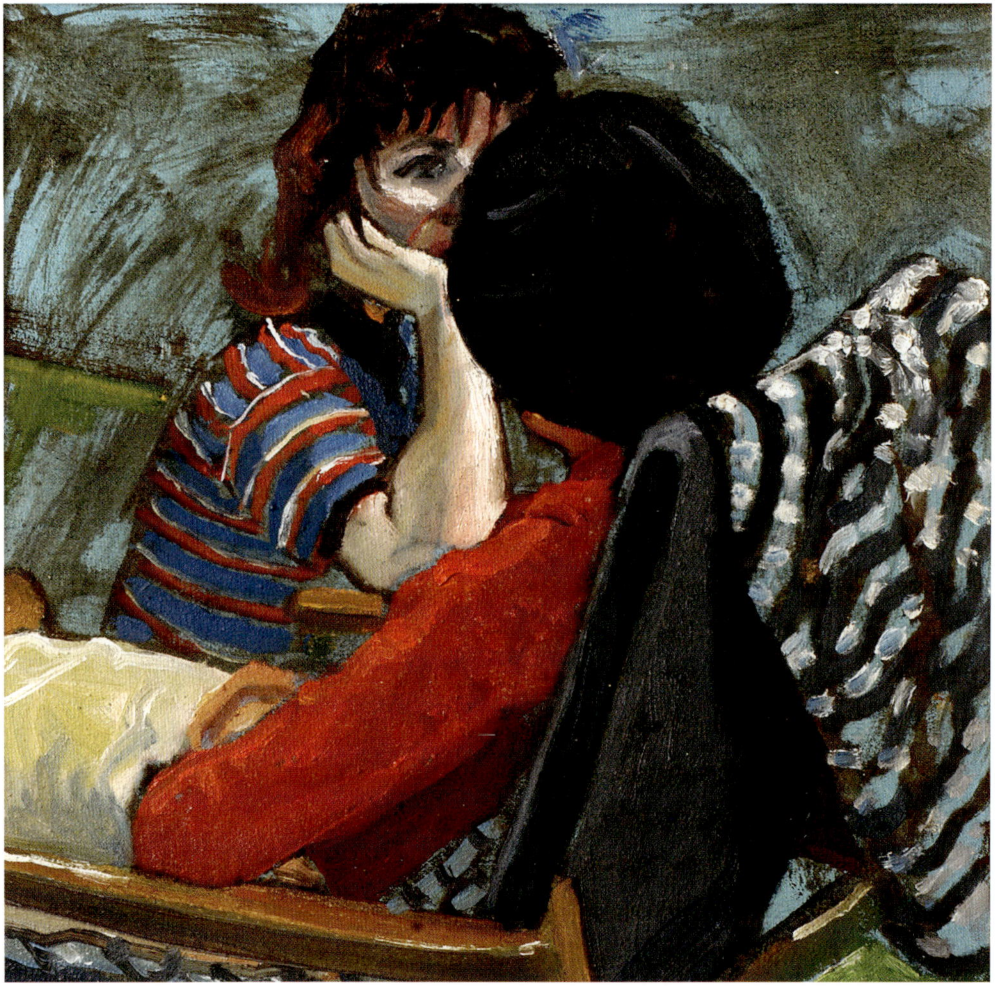

Our poster proclaims

Our poster proclaims:
Tea, coffee or squash
Or just friendship
Can be found in the parish hall
Round the corner,
Every Saturday from ten-fifteen
To twelve.

Not flaming passion, not love;
Nothing garish.
This is on the parish.
But quick-eyed friendship
Is waiting round the corner
With something warm,
Sweetened as required,
Lightened with the morning milk of kindness,
Where two or three are gathered together
On Saturdays from ten-fifteen to twelve.
Squeeze it in,
Squash it into your hour-glass,
Sandwich it between your shopping.
Come in, come in,
Sit down and rest your feet
Where refreshment is and friendship can
Be found,
And spoons with which to measure out
Your life;
Or to stir it up.
We may be just the stimulant you need,
Your cup of tea.
Or…we have a coffee-grinder
Or…just a friendly reminder.

Sun is ...

Sun is a morning blaze on blue
From which we flinch and shield our eyes.
It burns a cheek and warms a side
And lights a hemisphere of moon
Descending in the west.

Sun is the Horned One, Mithras, Odin,
Standing stones and sacrifice,
Solstice dawning, Celtic temples,
Saturnalia, Viking fear
And festivals of light.

Sun is a cipher, nothing, nought,
Exploding thermonuclear bombs
Of energy and heat and light
And wasting them on empty space
And eight dumb deities.

Sun is the power on Earth of one
Who stands upright; it counts for him,
This micro-macro mortal man
Who stores the sun's explosive power
And travels to the moon.

Sun is his life: his dark is death,
His earthy body casts a shade,
He warms his hands before the fire
And switches on the candle-power,
Scared of the dark and cold.

Sun is, and was, and while it lasts
Will spiral in the dust of stars
That twinkle in the galaxy,
One of a million million more
In endless noughts of space.

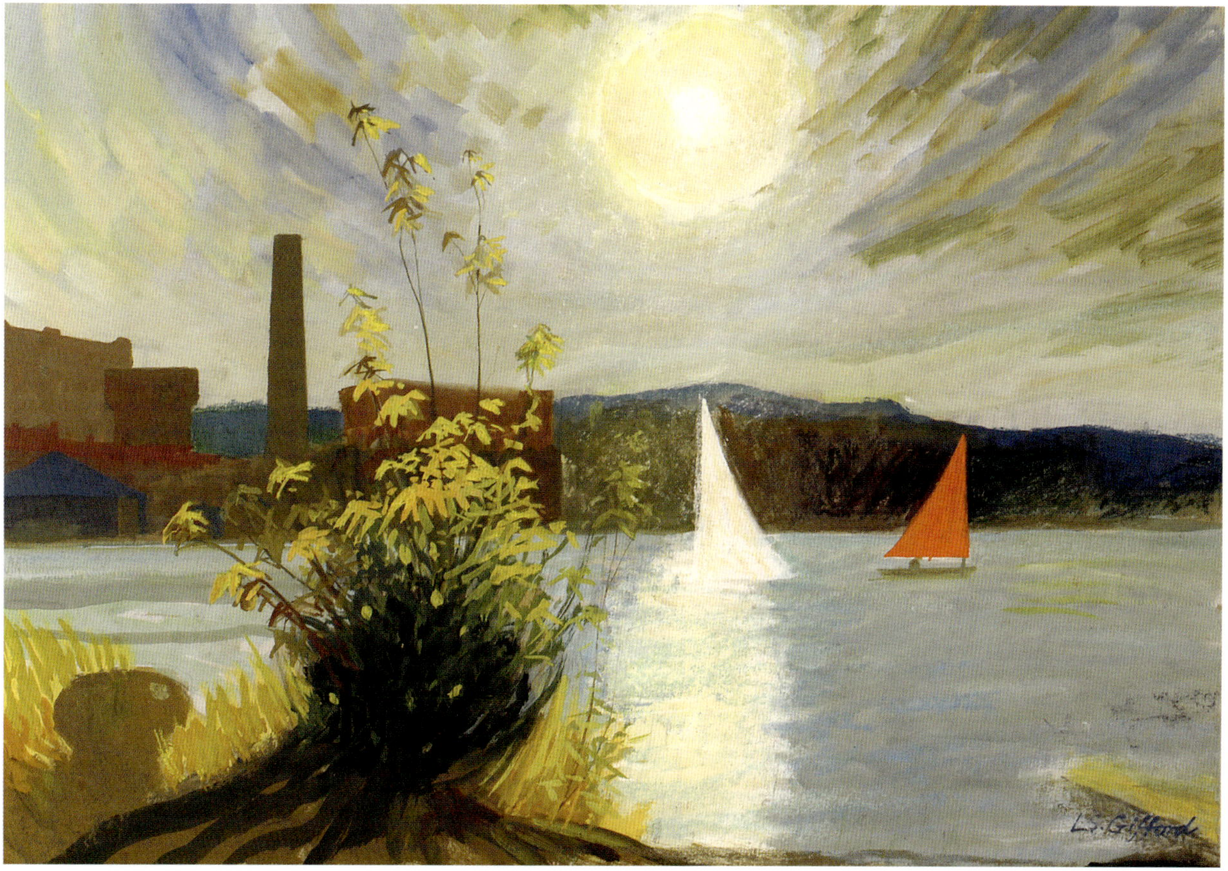

By my bean row

I sit relaxed today in my garden chair.
The sun at ten beats down on brow and brain
and roofs are dark against the blinding glare

where small still clouds string out across the blue.
A chestnut spear cuts through the red roof line
and bramble branches in thick fountains flow.

Two feet across, the rhubarb fans spread out.
Tomato fronds grow with the grace of elms
and colander-holed cabbages have taken heart.

My beans climb eight feet high over my head
on pointed arches of curving chestnut sticks,
a skeleton, fleshed now in green and red.

The fiery flowers catch everywhere in a blaze
that dies and flames all up the bright green wall:
bean embryos, finger-nail parings, take their place.

Beans touch red blobs in little weaving hops
and springy runners reach out like thin snakes.
Each growing head lazily lifts and dips.

I nursed them up, as each unguarded neck
and head appeared out of the April earth,
and sprinkled blue-green slug bait, tried to baulk

the night attacks of slugs intent to kill,
waiting to eat the latest tender stalk
before it spiralled upwards around a pole.

And now I feed and water and admire
my beans that race each other to the top
and past the top and higher still and higher.

In August and September life is strong,
and later flames appear along the row,
where giant fingers hang, cucumber-long.

until the sun no longer tops the sky
and growth grows weak along its weaker path,
and lingering the leaves begin to die.

Then, on a cooler day than this, I'll take
the dry corpse down and fling it on the fire
and watch red flowers climb up a wall of smoke.

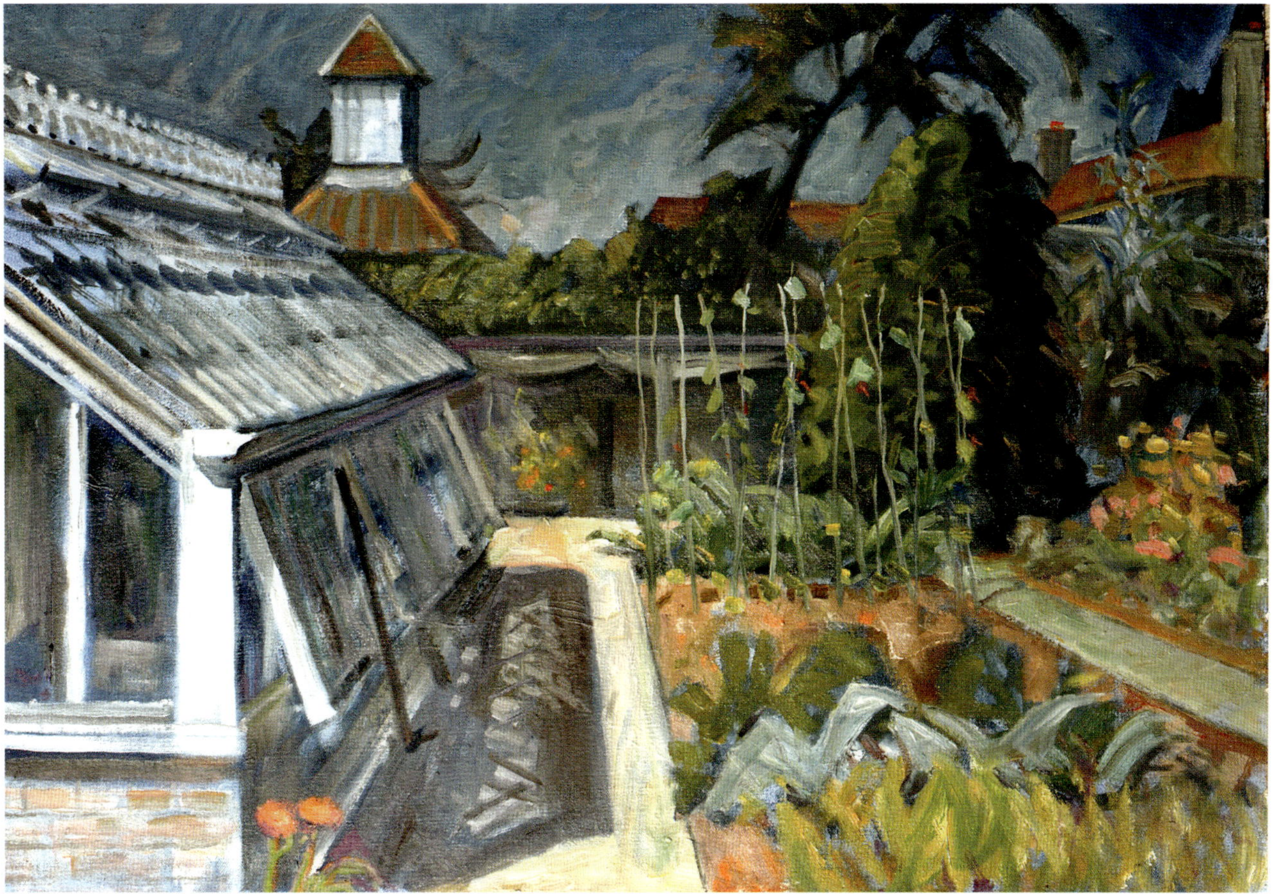

This Monday

This Monday is slipping away.
O why do I feel so weary?
And journeys to go, things to do,
And troublesome chores to get through.
A wall and a path to repair,
And a garden I try to ignore,
And muddles that never get straight,
A letter I promised to write,
And a library book to return.
It's twelve! – and I've hardly begun.
So what can be made of today?
I'll turn all things in my way
For now, into objets trouvés:
Assemble them into a theme,
A net made of rhymes to redeem
The wreckage adrift on the stream.

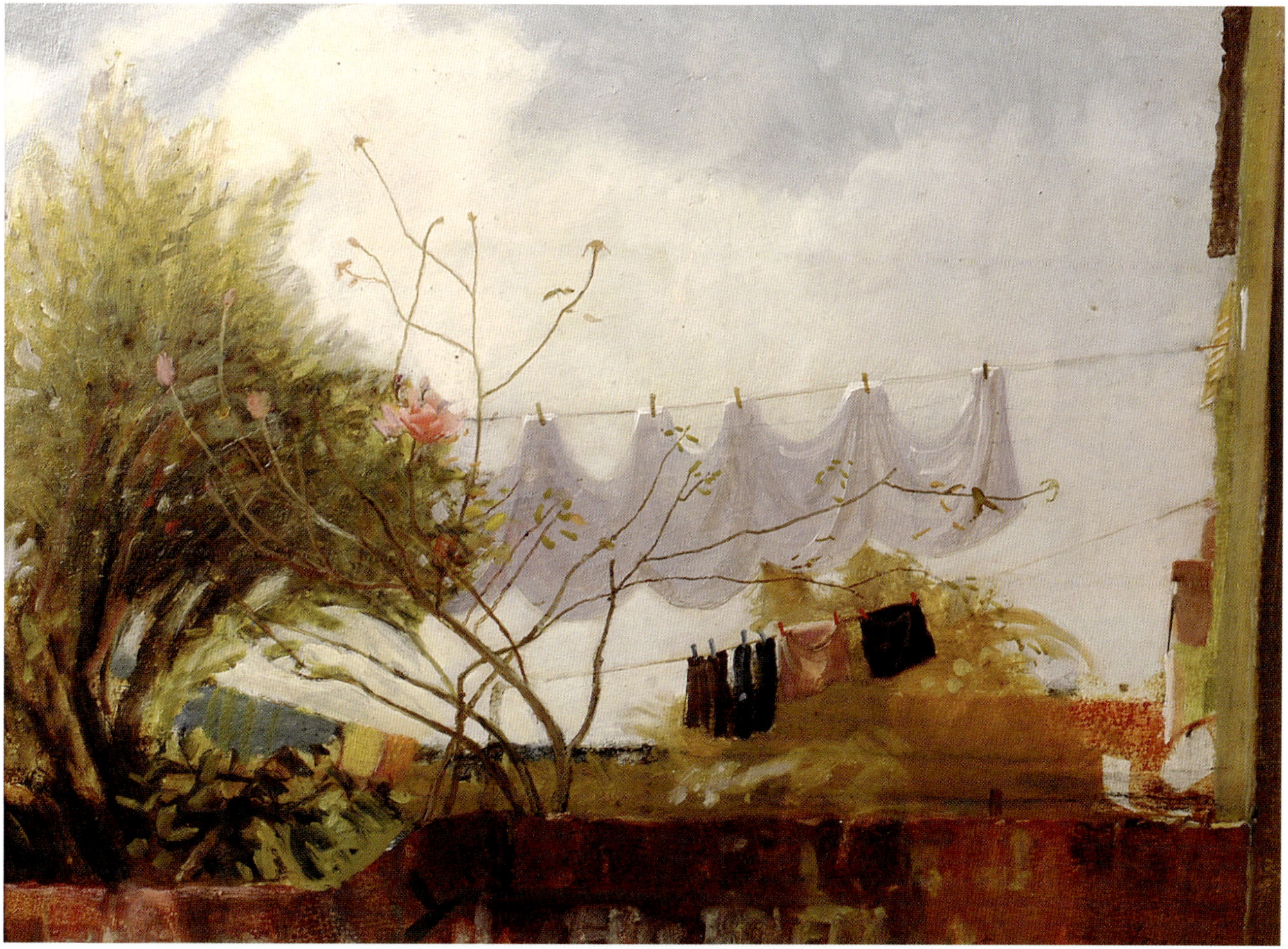

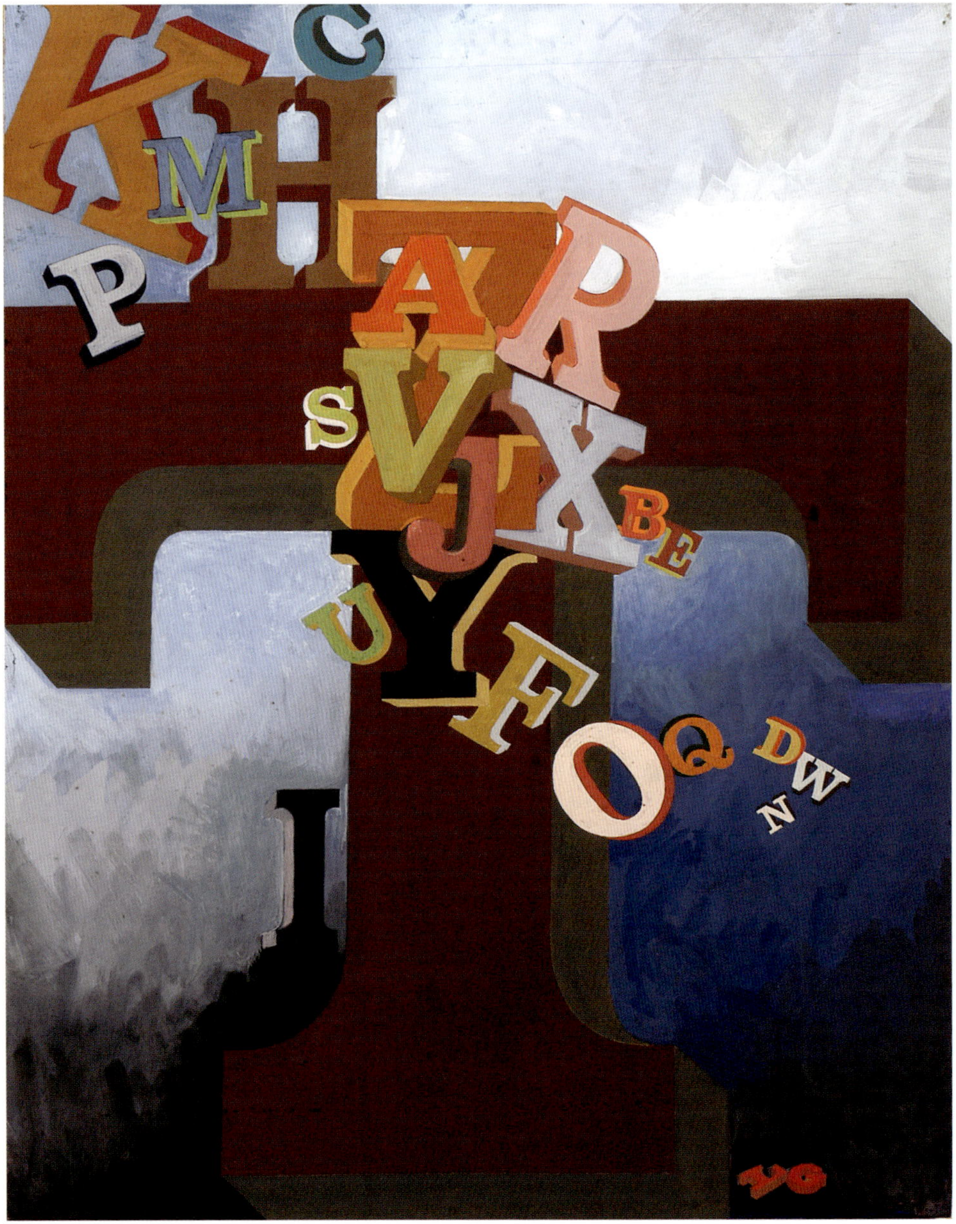

At the word painting class

How are you getting on?
Don't throw yourself on the canvas.
You have to choose
From this colour-box of words.
From Chambers and Roget's.
And remember,
Sober palettes are the most expressive.
Let your lines flow into each other
Or meet in angular shock.
Give your work shape and power.
These details that you've spent much time on –
Put your brush through them,
They're not essential.
Watch your phonetics;
These plosive sounds just here are rather strong;
Too strong. Too stressed.
This is where you need them.
Hold consonants piled up
In orange-red strength
Against those blue-green vowels.
Soften your edges here:
Drag your brush lightly along
With alliteration.
That's better. Are you happy with it?
No? Then leave off. Have a whisky
And come back.
You may see then what you have to do.
But don't give up.
Think of the sheer joy when it all comes right.
Sometimes it all comes right.

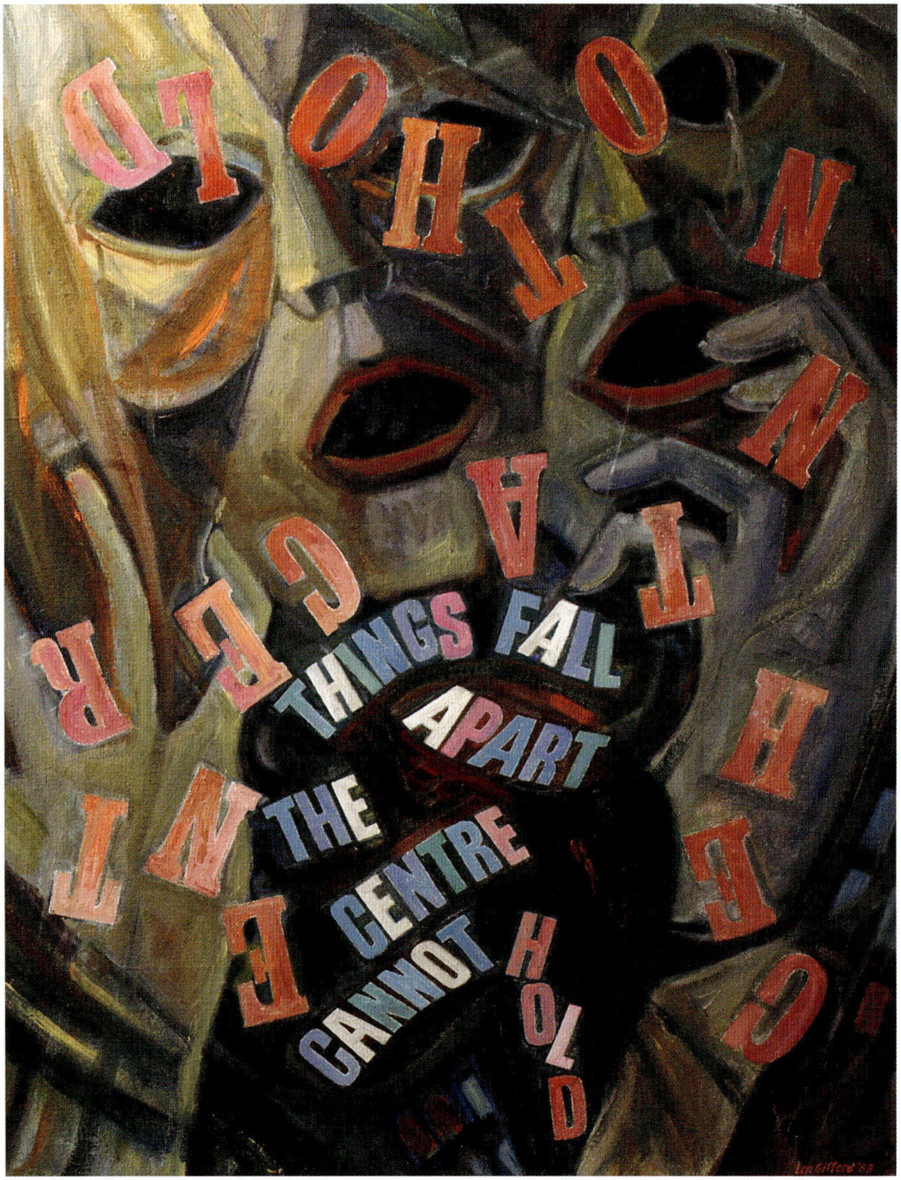
THINGS FALL
APART
THE
CENTRE
CANNOT
HOLD

How easel was chosen

It came to pass, the Lord of Alphabets
Took up his pencil and put forth his hand
And struck the printed page of Universe
At random in the Anglo-Saxon zone.
By chance it was the planet Epsilon,
The fifth one of the twenty-six that stretched
From Alpha through to Zeta. People said
This was a seismic shock: others believed
The Lord of Letters wished to raise a great
Prophet of the Epsilonians who
Would rule the tribes; the Verbs, the Adjectives,
The Nouns, the Pronouns and the Adverbs too.
But *these* were not the words the people used.
And why not? – you may ask. Be patient still.
Soothsayers *said* that he would be a Noun.
And they were right. Easel the son of Elm
Had had a dream. A great and roving Eye
Had fixed on him: an astral voice had said:
'Speak to the Epsilonians in their tongue'...
Which Easel did. His picture of the world
Because the only words his listeners knew,
The only words that they could understand,
Began with 'E'. His picture of the world
Was limited. But Easel did his best.
'Endure!', he said, 'episodes existential,
Events eluding easy explanation,
Embracing earnestly extra-terrestrial
Exceedingly effulgent expectations!'
And so, of course, for cryptic words like these
Easel was honoured, *even* in his own land.

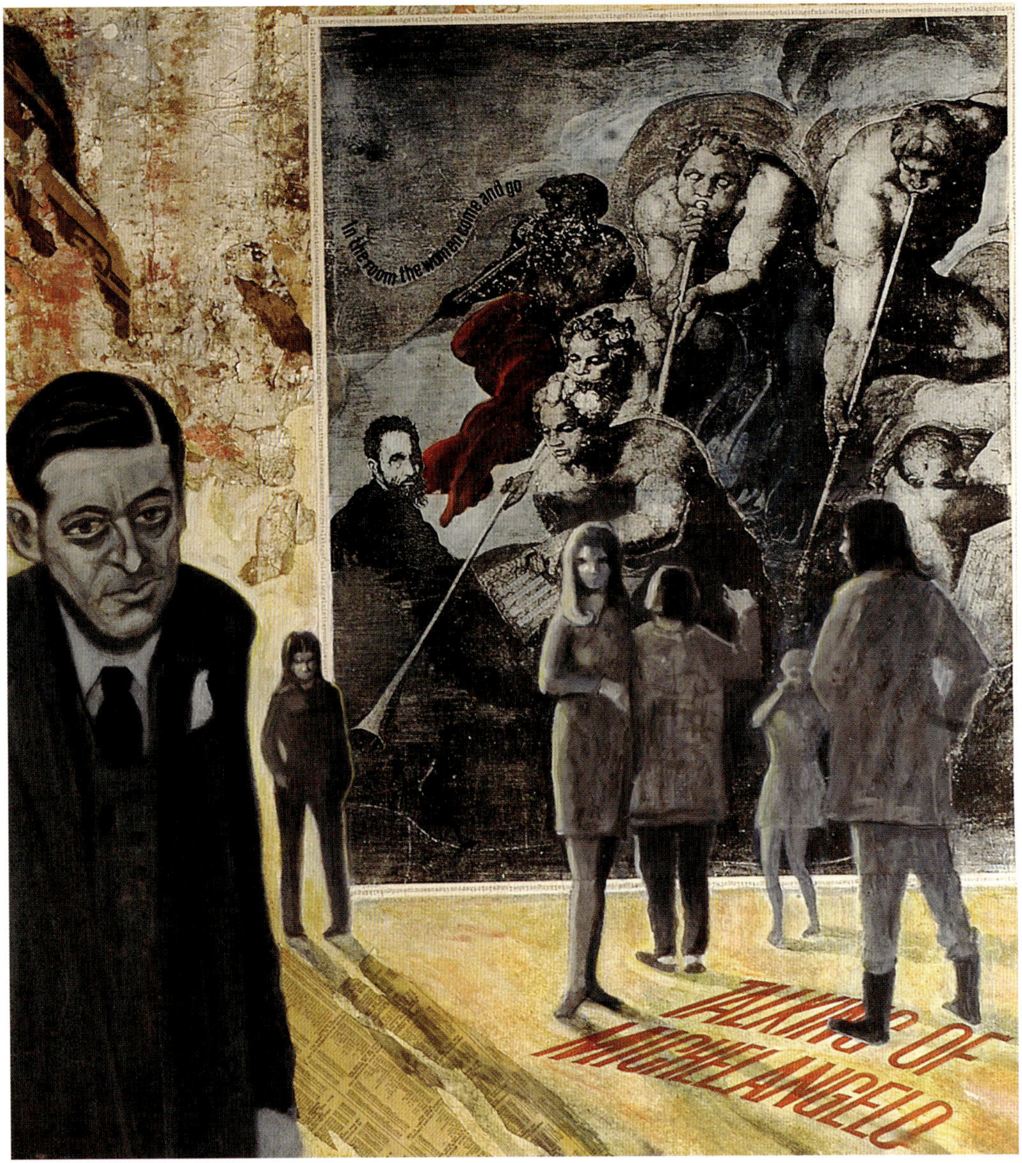
In the room the women come and go
TALKING OF
MICHELANGELO

For us there is only the trying

If you could only say to yourself: 'After breakfast
I shall carry on painting the Sistine Chapel
Or, I shall finish off the Mona Lisa
Or, p'raps I ought to begin on my Ninth...'

But no. You'll sit and watch your uffish thoughts
Go pale and sink and die in the sluggish stream.

Have you ever watched how peas in water
Lie on the bottom quietly till the heat
Moves one, or three or four, and then they rise
Like little rescued souls until at last
Every one twists and turns in a riotous dance?

You have to wait like this – numb – cold,
And rub two sticks together for a flame
And be prepared and watch
For a thought to rise,
For a word to join a word and make a phrase,
For a line to join a line to make a verse,
For verses linked together in the dance.

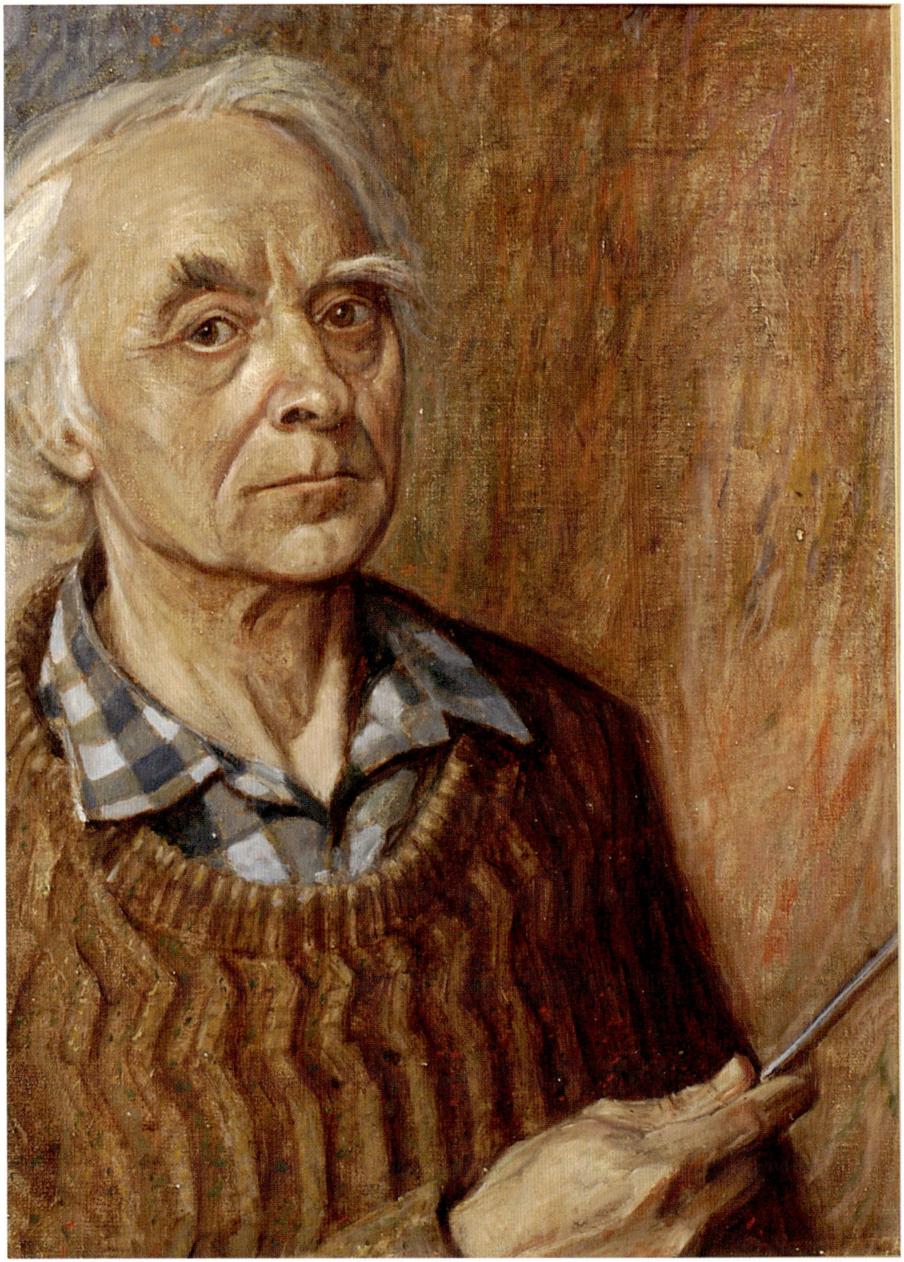

A formal dance

Sestinas have six stanzas of six lines.
They would just about
Be eligible, typed, but not in long-hand
For National Poetry Competitions. Their shape
Is strict. The six words at the end
Repeat in every stanza, changing place.

And this is where a change of word takes place
And all six words appear on different lines
And all these words are in a triplet at the end.
Words change about
Like a set of bells or dance of formal shape.
It's limiting – but on the other hand

It's like a painter, free, with brush in hand
Whose only discipline is to fill a place
In a certain frame of arbitrary shape.
No verse is free. Some poems follow lines
Not hedged about
With any formal structure. But their end

Though reached by different means, is the same end;
Sometimes even from the self-same hand
Experiment, new form, a face-about,
Untyped, uncategoried, hard to place,
With meanings caught in tortured twisted lines
Can scare the critics with its menacing shape.

Choosing words – testing the taste and shape
Of sounds on the palate or at the tongue's end –
The rhythm of lines
Firm or lightly sketched with a tentative hand
Moving about on work-sheets from place to place
Is what it's about.

Trial and error – Ah! but what about
Inspiration – is the Muse's shape
Hovering gracefully in her proper place
Coaxing the wayward quill to a tasteful end?
She's there – bestowing with her other hand
Her mean reluctant quota of quotable lines.

Now at the end, six words have changed about
By sleight-of-hand to make this special shape
On ancient lines in modern time and place.

Villanelle for a villainy

'Lady fall out!' the howling infant said.
    'O Johnny love, we're talking. Can't you see?'
'Window! A bad man pushed her. Is she dead?'

    The mother idly stroked the little head
    and poured herself another cup of tea.
'Lady fall out!' the howling infant said.

    'Now don't go on – you'll only make me mad.
    Stop it! Your father wants to talk to me.'
'Window! A bad man pushed her. Is she dead?'

    The mother cut another slice of bread
    and heard the noise of words, but absently.
'Lady fall out!' the howling infant said.

    His voice was getting hoarse, and his face red.
    He thrashed about and pointed stubbornly.
'Window! A bad man pushed her. Is she dead?'

    His father turned to him. 'It's time for bed.
    What was that dreadful fuss about, my boy?'
'Lady fall out!' the howling infant said.
'Window! A bad man pushed her. Is she dead?'

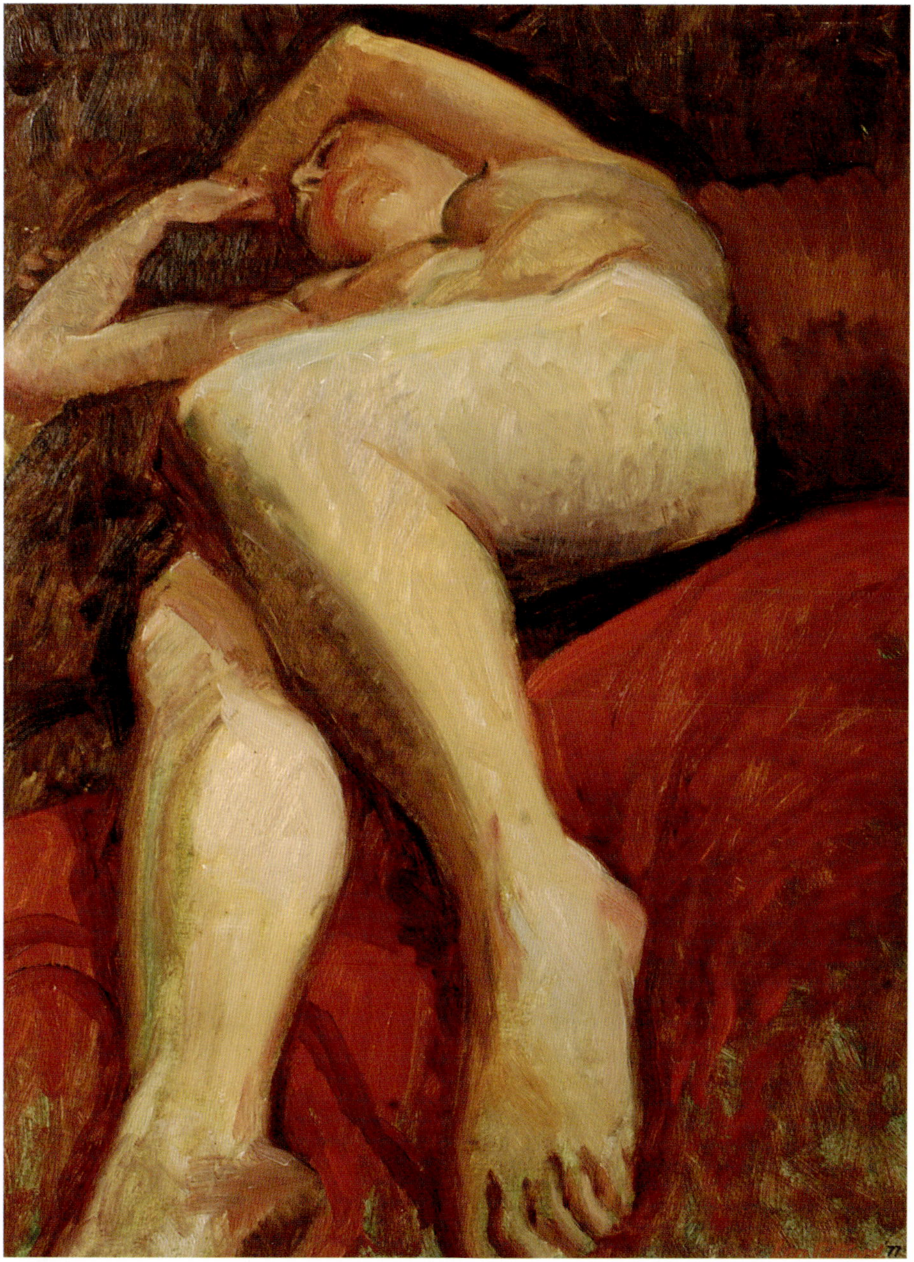

Colours

They come in the warp of the world,
in the weft of the world
as a gift of light,
gift of the sun and moon.
They glimmer on the hour-hand of clocks at dawn,
glow on the minute-hand
flash and flame in full light.
The round world wears a Joseph's coat
belted with rainbows.
Creation is chromatic.
They are the index and power of Nature,
the love of painters,
for Monet, portraying the gradations of decay
on Camille's dead face, a drug,
stronger than love.
They are the dyer's delight, the printer's passion,
the stuff of theatre,
triumph of the tube, splendour of the screen,
majesty of banners, panoply of priests,
beauty of bouquets, glory of gardens,
boon of the brash young, who turn them on
full volume.
They are the forte of
women everywhere, who understand them.
The language of words knows their weight and sway.
Who would dismiss them as cosmetic,
because they are on the surface?
They pierce, like a whisper, a shout, a
touched string, a struck key,
straight down through the heart.

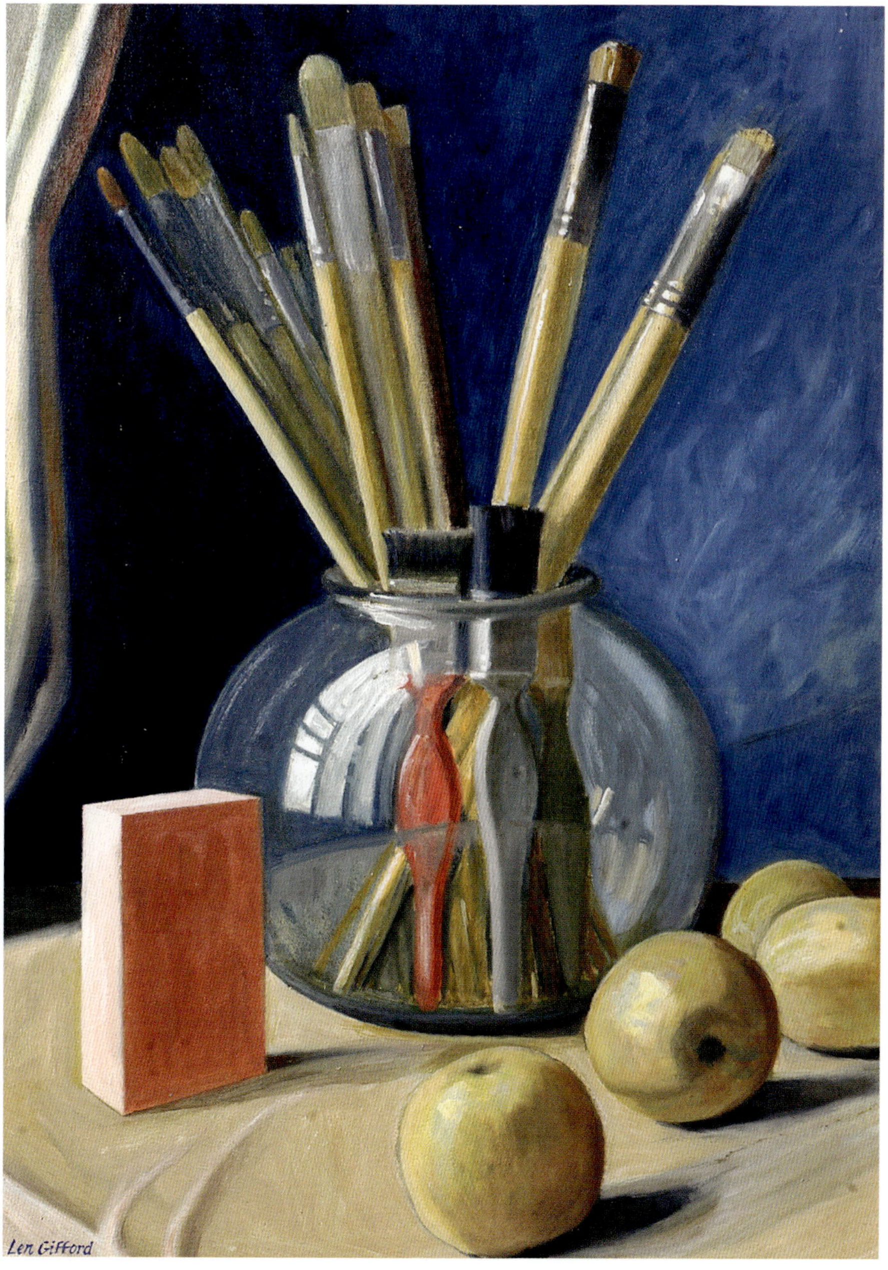
Len Gifford

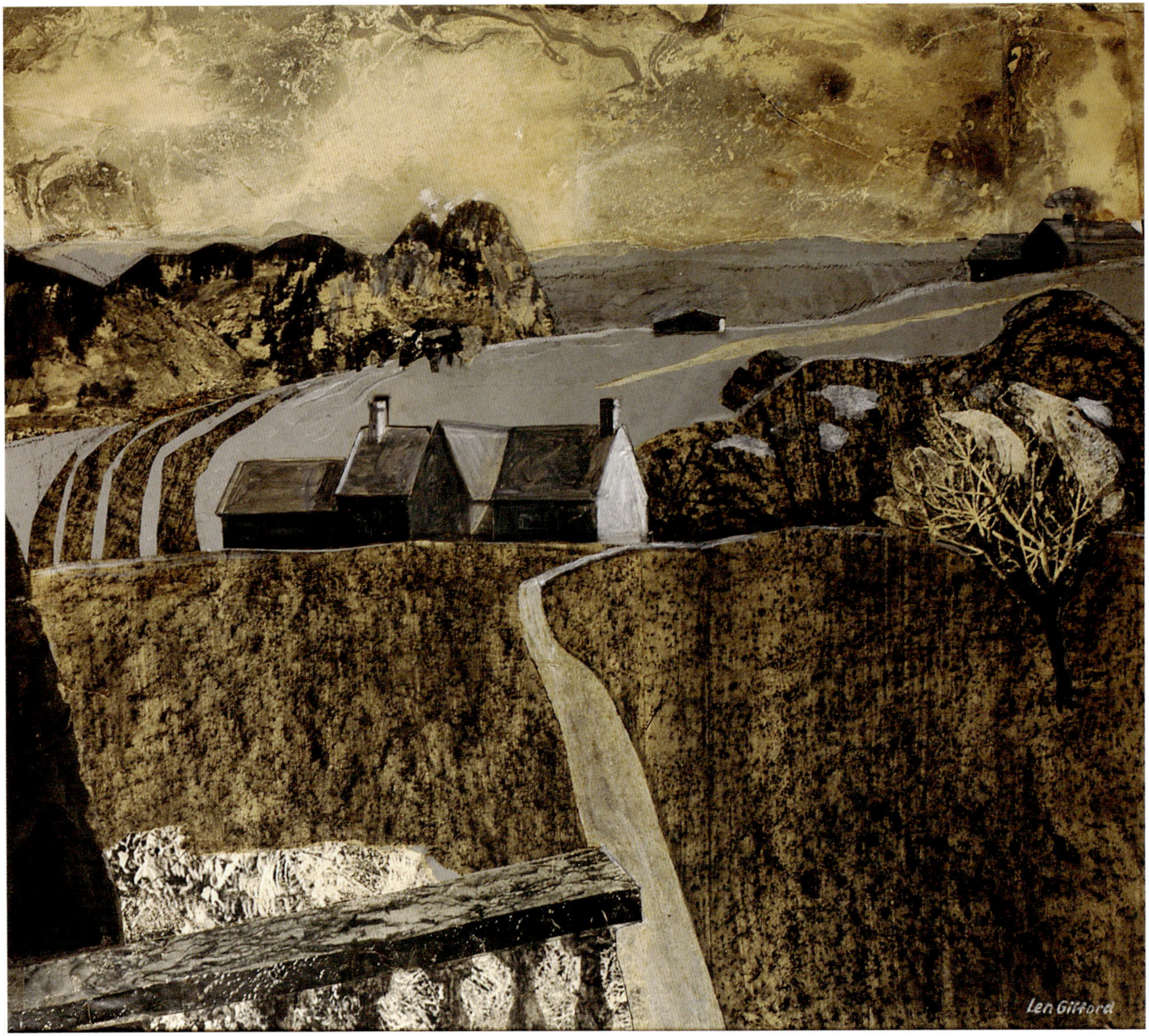
Len Gifford

Landscape in Grisaille

Colour is – ornament? Display?
    What if the day was dark or bright
But every tone was neutral grey,
    Or charcoal through to Chinese white,
    From dawn to dullest dead of night –
Could we endure such lives of lead?
    Would we remember old delight
When skies were blue and blood was red?

Even the sun's moon-silvered ray
    Could not abate our bitter plight
What would we write or think or say:
    How could we stay our starveling sight
    In cities shrouded, sick with fright –
Grey-black, grey-white, – nothing instead?
    Paradise was before the blight,
When skies were blue and blood was red.

How like a stone the world would weigh
    Between black seas and steely height!
Grey buds, grey blossoms, grass and hay –
    Creation robbed of appetite
    Afraid to sip or suck or bite
Baulking at bread, dry-mouthed with dread,
    Denied the joy of that birthright
When skies were blue and blood was red.

Envoi

    Would human nature be contrite,
And thankful, every heart and head –
    To see again the common light
When skies were blue and blood was red?

The poetry of inanimate objects

Oh dear! What can the matter be?
What can it *not* be? Simple mind
Muddled with its complexity

By things of every shape and kind
Thinks that the apple on the plate
Lies still. But common sense is blind.

The whole darned world is animate,
Frightful with energy. En masse
A weapon with atomic weight

Moving in solids, water, gas –
Spontaneous in radium.
And mad plutonium particles

Generate pandemonium.
Lessons in physics may create
An element of tedium.

I only say senses can cheat.
Tables and chairs, my pen, this room
All move – they're not inanimate.

Nor earth, nor clouds, nor sun, nor moon,
Nor all that nature pushes up,
Nor all that gravity brings down,

Nor man (embracing woman), whose scope
Is wider than the world of things.
A creature of despair and hope
Who still believes he holds the strings.

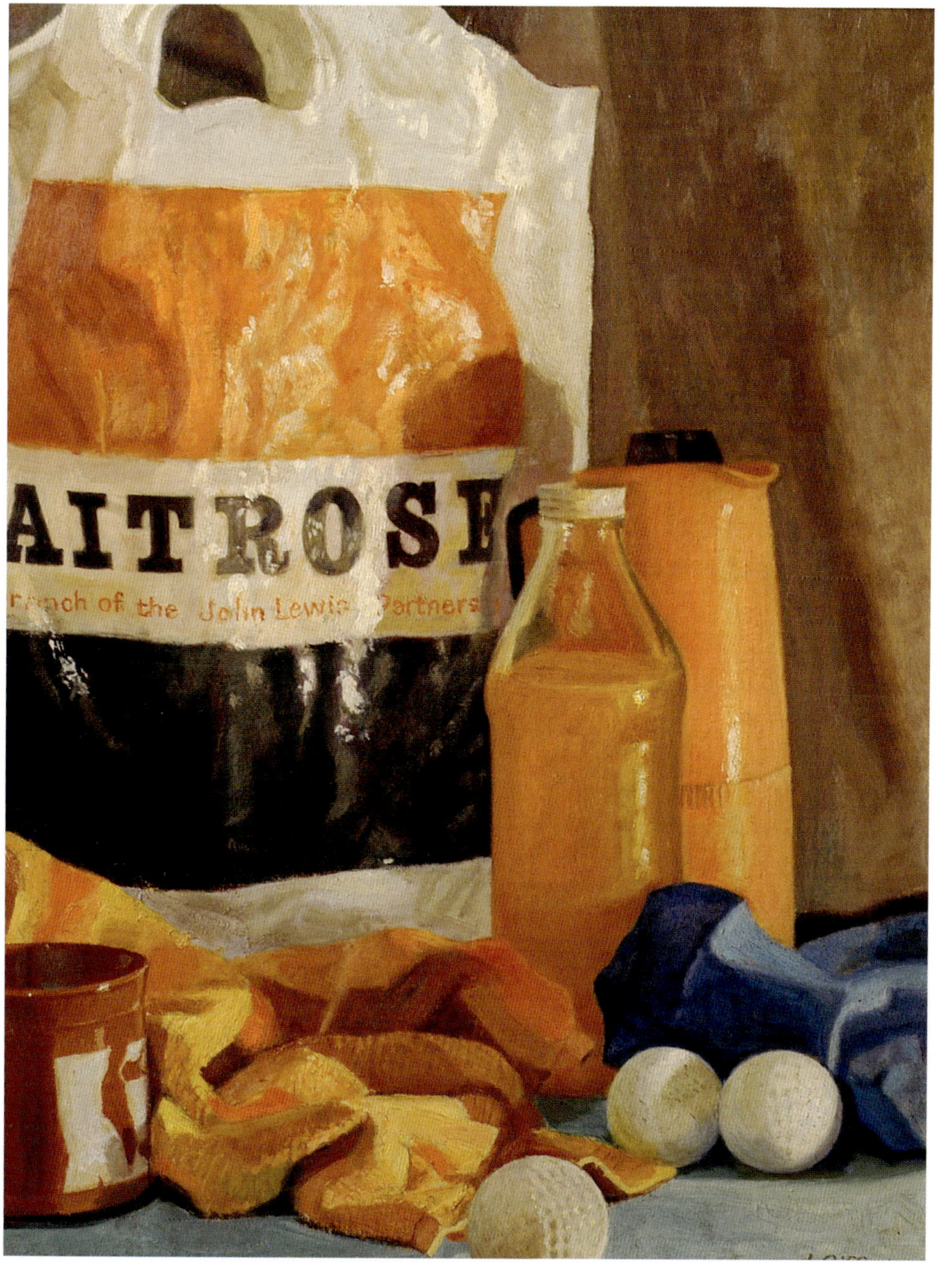
AITROSE

The world of Odilon Redon

What has my devilish charcoal drawn?
Ten legs surround a lump of coal.
A hairy spider, with a smile
That scuttles round and round my brain.
I slip from terra firma's edge
To monstrous seas. In fancy's swell
What lies on that low pedestal?
A bowl that holds a martyred head.
As though it watched the infinite
An up-turned eye and eye-ball soars
Balloon-like. From converging cords
A pudding face stares from a plate.
A goblin's head blocks out the sun.
It ponders ocean's mysteries
With big and bulbous, thoughtful eyes,
And hangs upon a tiny wing.
A hollow head that lacks a jaw,
This head upon a neck of bone,
A rope that fleshless hands pull on.
A bell that swings and sounds a knell.
Inside a curve of fleshy stalk
An eye, hypnotic, looks and lours.
If Alice dreamed of this, her flowers
Would be too mortified to speak.
A passing cyclops stops and looks
And ogles with his single eye
A careless girl or goddess who
Reclines upon the flowers and rocks.
And flowers in a simple vase
Explode with pyrotechnic might
And fall in showers of coloured light
In vivid pastels, vibrant oils.
The painter, with eclectic eye
Transmutes the world, its grist and grain
In the intestine of his brain
To prodigy, monstrosity.

Inside my skull, with scuttering feet
The spiders spin their webs and wait.

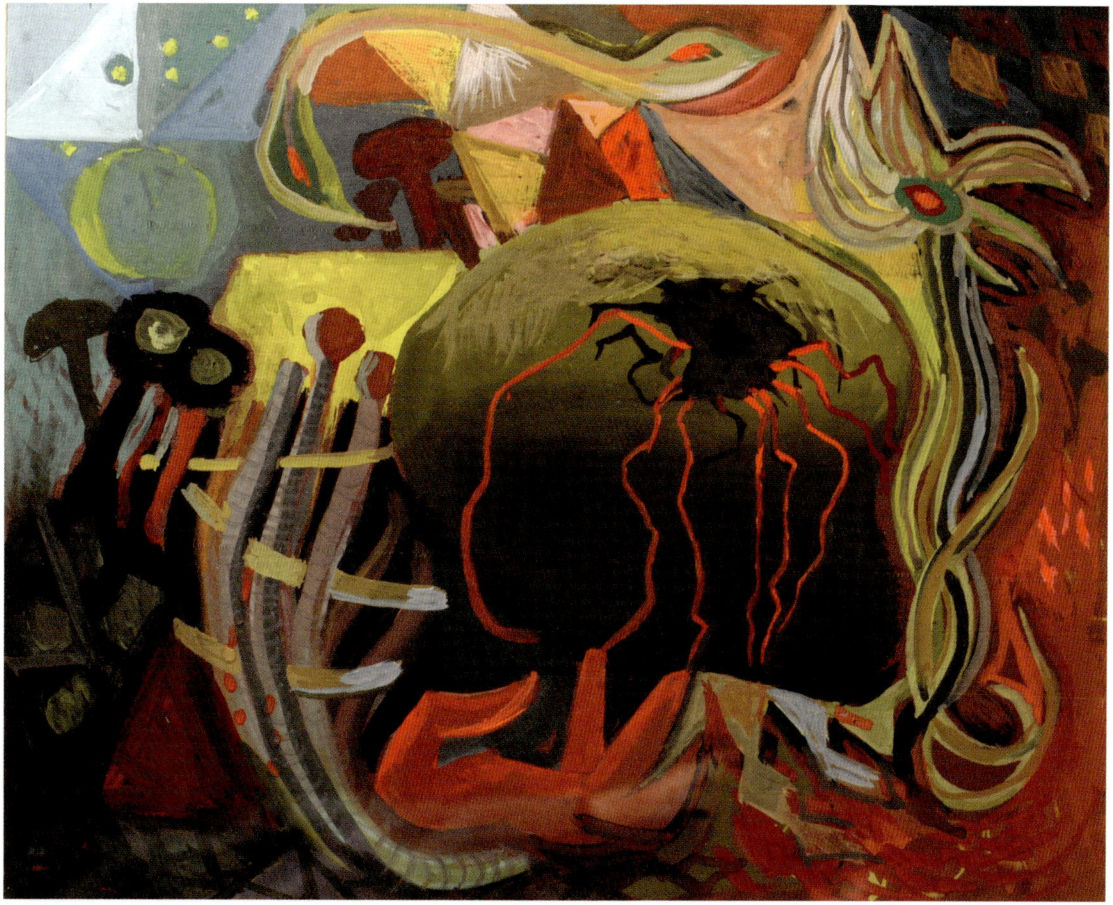

Easton before the Freeway

The tractors came. My street has gone.
The room where I was born is now
conceptual, above a road,
and all the houses are laid low
and lost beneath a tyre-borne flood.
More than a generation on,

From something not entirely lost
I try to summon yesterday.
I see the place I knew, again.
Like positives left in the tray
the pictures sharpen in my brain
across a tower block, looming vast.

Then, sepia thoughts of Easton fade
before the new Bristolians
with braided hair, in Eastern dress
and darker skins. They shop at Singh's
emporium of specialities
close to the inner circuit road,

Close to the echoing underpass.
And yet, today, Easton enjoys
what its betters took for granted
up in Clifton and Henleaze,
smarter houses, gardens planted,
playing fields and trees and grass.

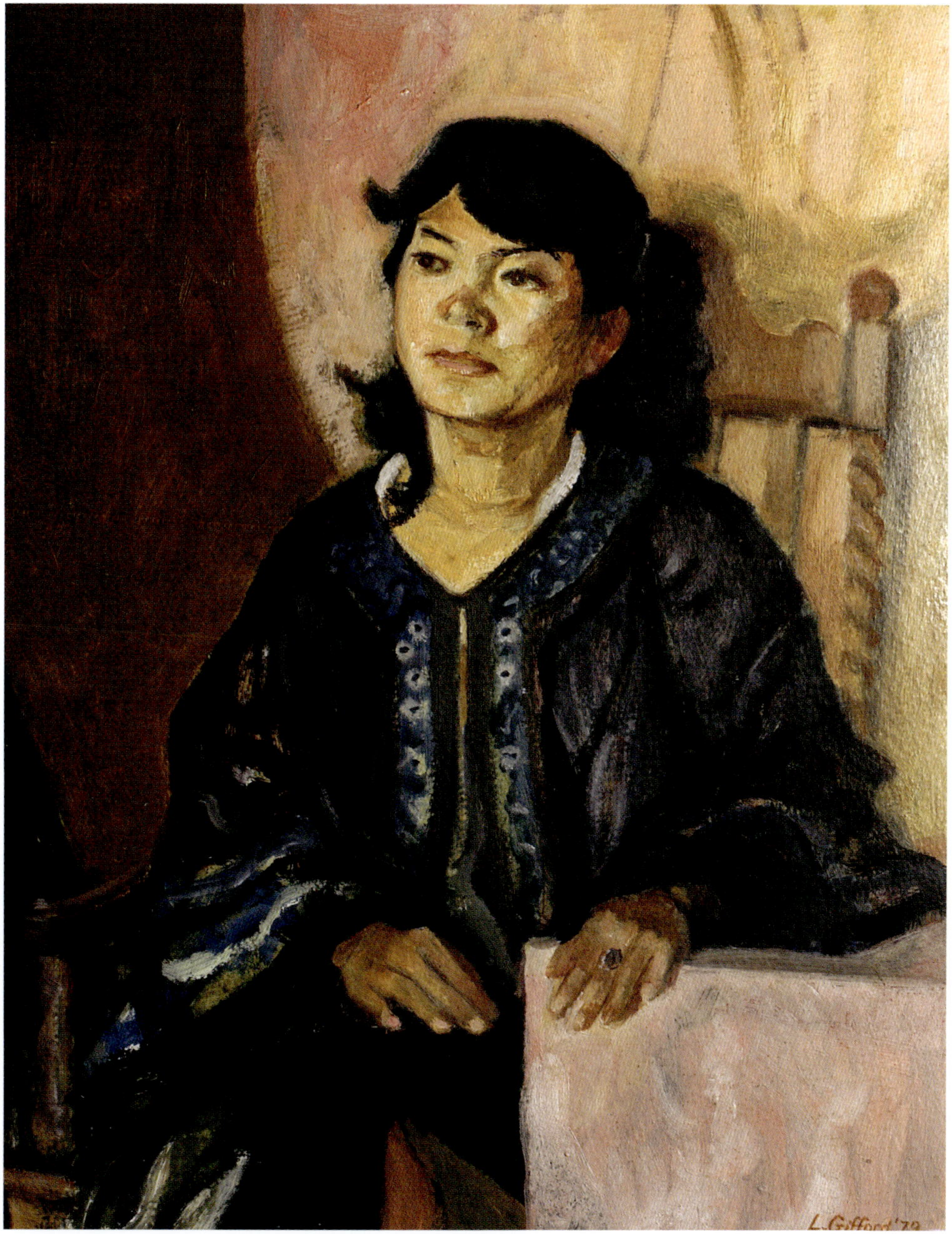
L.Gifford

Our lodger

What wind in what willows
Brings back the smell of home?
I tunnel down through misremembered years
To three great-aunts, Liz and Sal and Flo
Not counting Sophie, who died,
Leaving behind a husband – Uncle Fred.

Fred was fond of his pipe and 'baccy.
He had a straggly moustache,
A spittoon,
And a creamy-white Pomeranian, Shacky,
Which was named after Sir Ernest
 Shackleton, much in the news.

He cleaned his oil-lamp chimney with
Screeching twists of newspaper.
Then we sat in the warm lamp-light
On the rag rug by the fire, snugly
In his bed-sit basement den
And when he dozed, with chin dropping down,

We would open his magazines,
Harmsworth Histories of the World,
Full of engravings printed
In purples or tasteful browns.
Pictures of palm trees, ziggurats
And Sardanapalus on his funeral pyre.

Fred was in the decorating trade,
Though his hand always trembled a little.
Perhaps it helped when he
Imitated wood-grain with special combs,
Or painted stone,
Cunningly, so that it looked like marble.

When we moved, to another old house,
I watched him slapping on wallpaper,
Tearing it with abandon to fit uneven walls.
I remember the bare sounding floor-boards,
And sleeping in a new bedroom
Shining and smelling with new paint.

Deep in the tunnel of memory,
Down among the half-remembered years,
The feel of things comes back, the taste,
The smell.
I could have mentioned other things instead.
I don't know why I'm stuck with Uncle Fred.

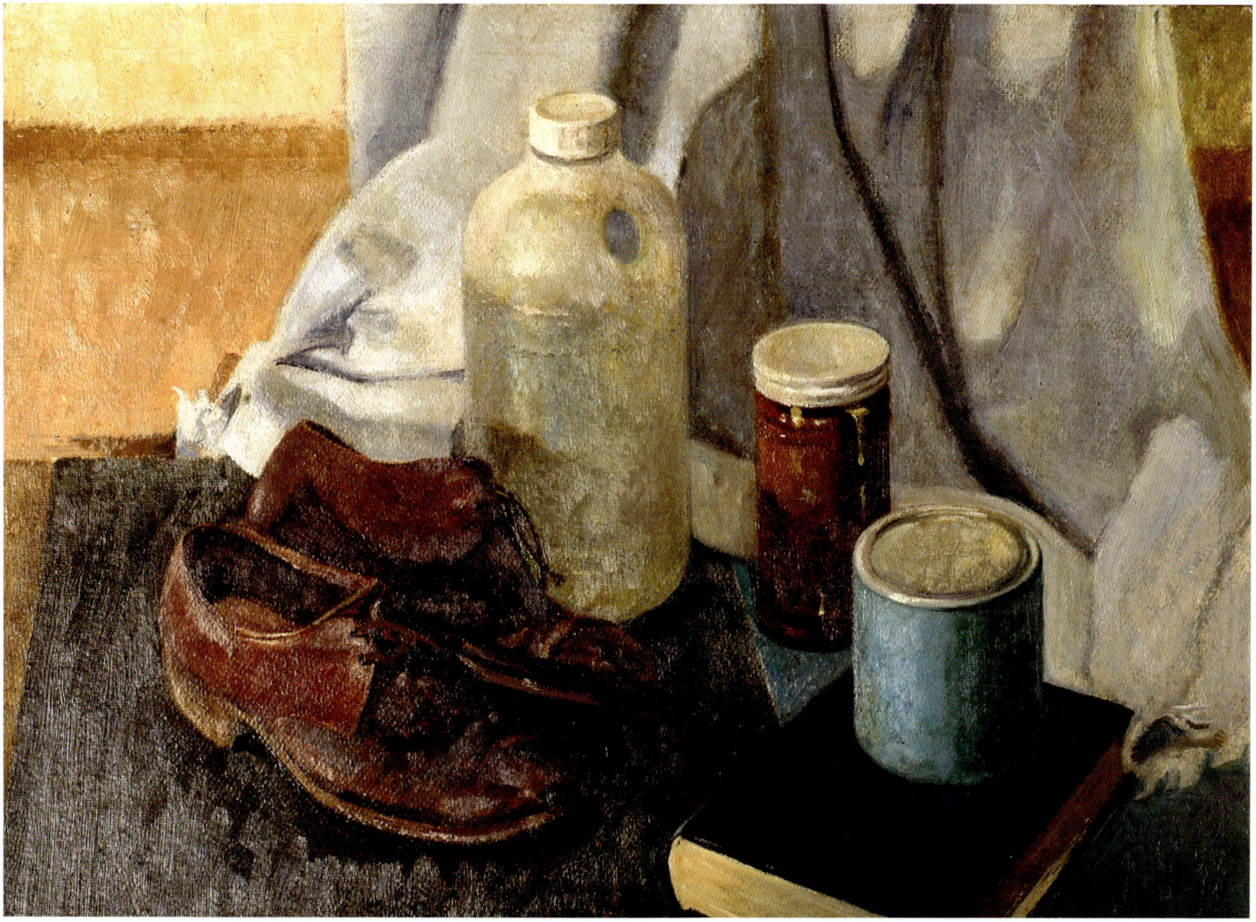

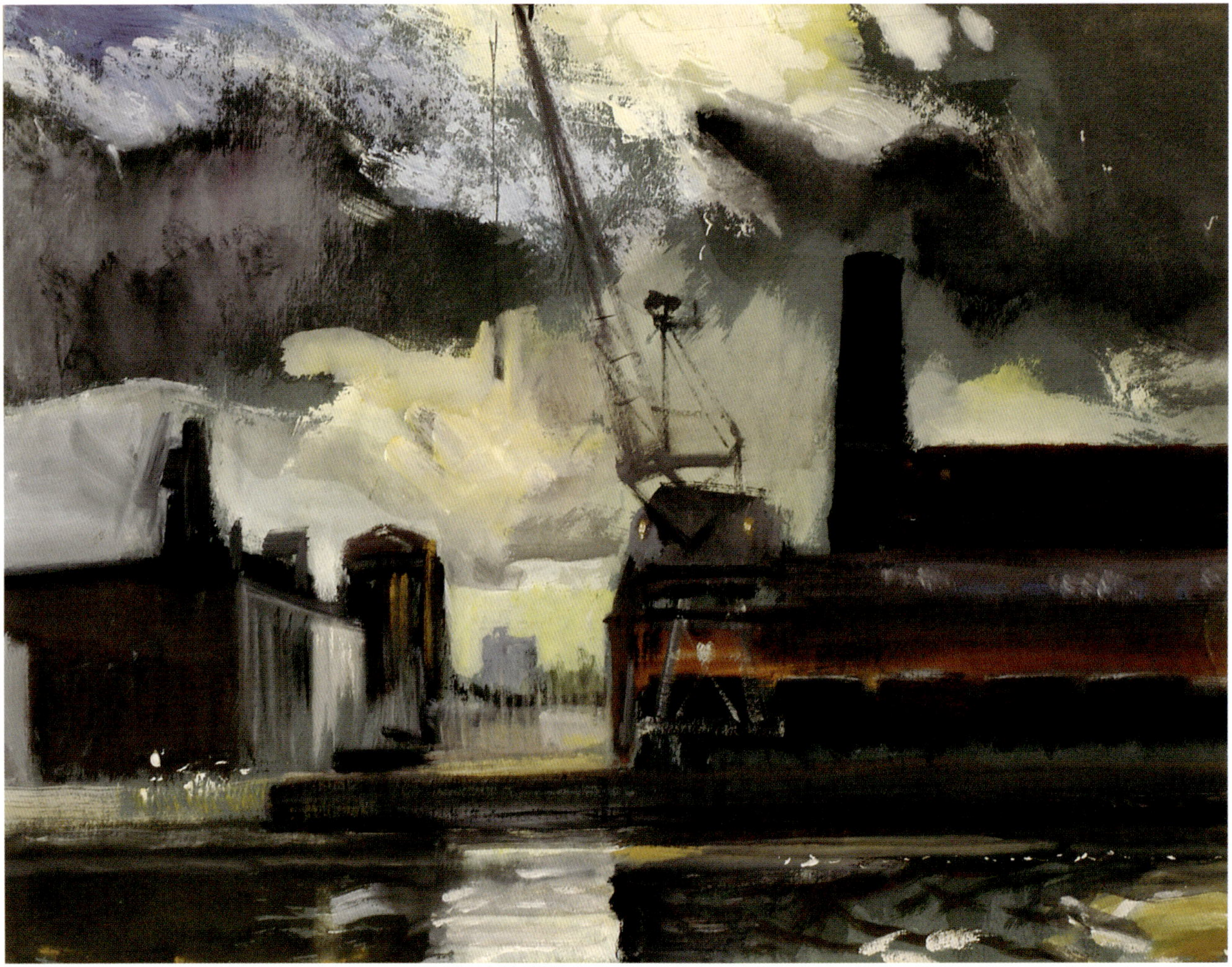

The Index

What begins with an Abbey – ends with Zion
honours the saints from Agnes to St. Werburgh,
echoes an ancient history – Corn and Wine,
Avon, Horsefair, Merchant and Old Market;
Authors and Musicians, (an assortment) –
Dickens, Emerson, Ruskin and Macaulay,
Holst and Elgar, Purcell, Stainer, Tallis,
and some poets, Betjeman and Chaucer,
Causley and Sassoon – As well as Shakespeare;
Where will you find the frankly euphemistic
Clover Field and Applegate and Birdwood,
Where World's End and There And Back Again,
Pinkham's Twist and Little Paradise?
These are the names of streets and roads and villas,
groves and gardens, avenues and crescents
over Greater Bristol's twenty regions,
over all the spreading conurbation,
over all the pious and industrious
patriotic, culture-conscious city –
ancient, modern, busily-building BRISTOL.

Bristoll, Citty and County

Bristol remembers its shape, the old linkage
Retraced in archives, in harbour and bridges
In that old England familiar to Chaucer.
Sailing on still – this merchantman riding
Terrestrial tides of our turbulent happenings
Over six hundred years since she was famously
Launched by King Edward, Plantagenet monarch.

Bristol remembers it – second to old London.
Recollects Cabot's departure down Avon
In little *Matthew*; remembers the traders.
Slowly restores I.K.Brunel's *Great Britain*,
Treasures old Temple Meads and the bridge hanging
Over the gorge. And many remember the
Lumbering trundling open-top tramcars.

Bristol refashions its star team of leaders!
Round the rink, on the court – Cousins and Durie,
In summer skies see the big balloons lifting,
See Concorde cutting the clouds and time speeding
To westwards where once the old packets were plying.
Old merchants, yesterday's eager adventurers
Linking with new-shaped endeavours tomorrow.

Bristol, reshaped, is still turning out leaders!

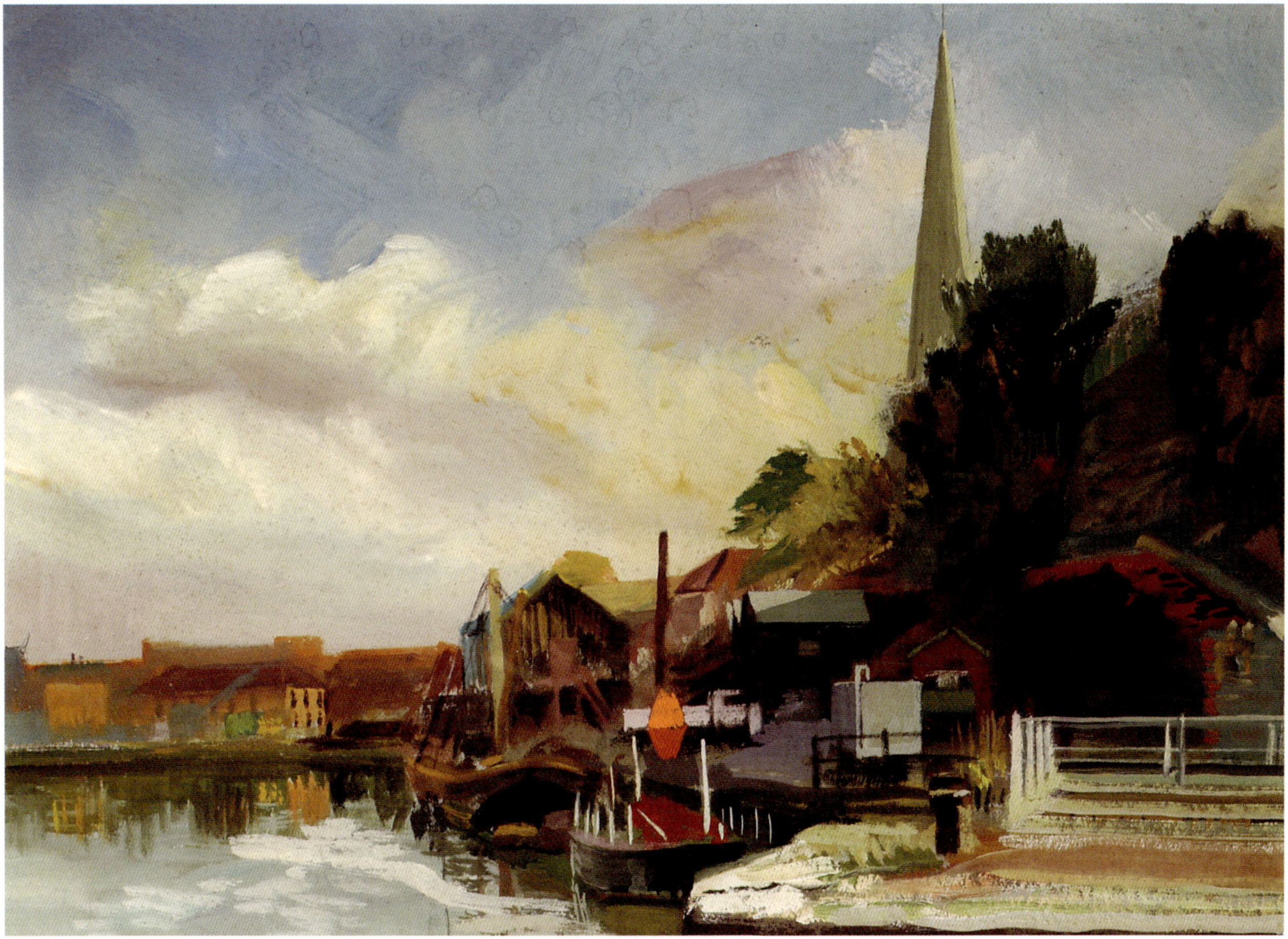

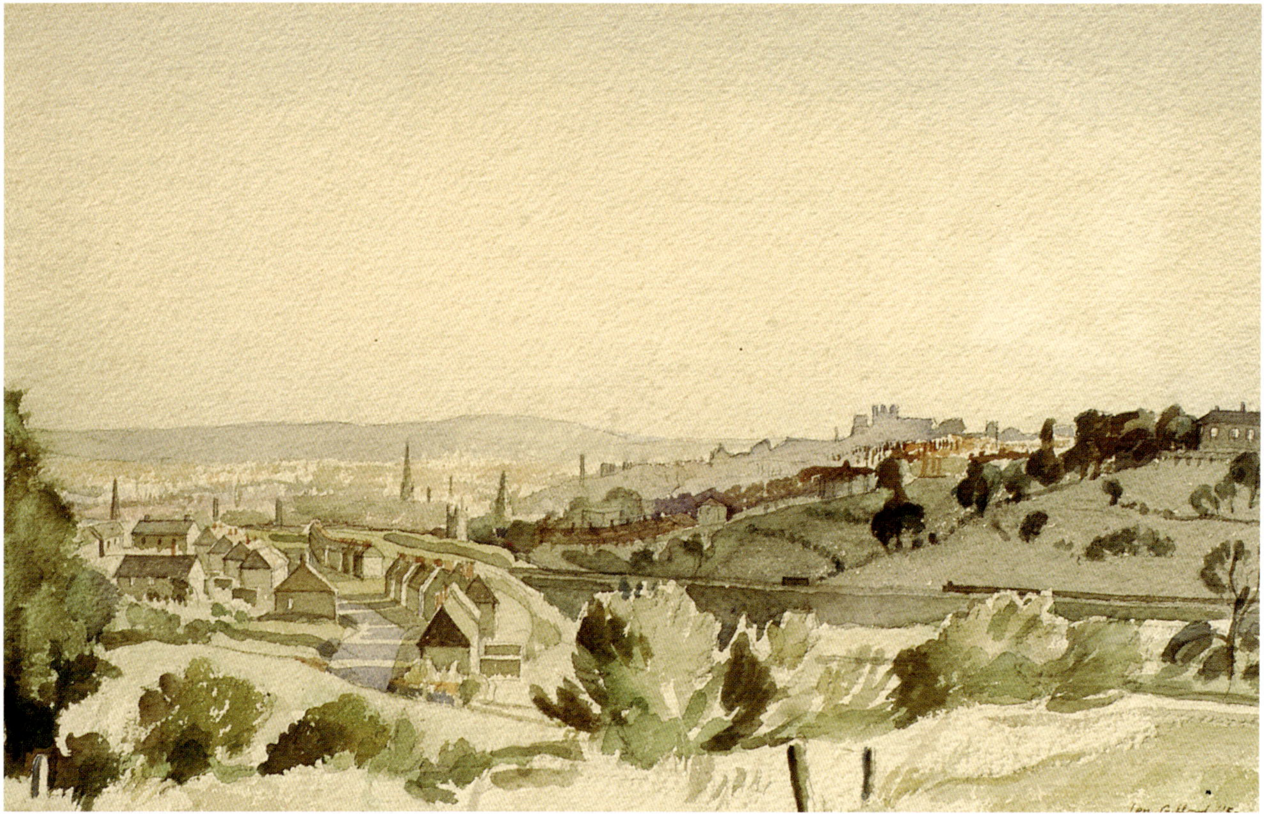

After listening to Mahler's 'Titan' Symphony

Sometimes life says: 'Hip Hooray'
with a painting, with a poem
or with music's alchemy.
Speeds our ship along with gold
on the decks and in the hold
and Apollo at the helm.

Probing down, the symphony's
strings in grave adagios
move our sensibilities.
Mere intestines of dumb sheep!
Why so eloquent and deep?
These and the woodwinds' arias

Touch a nameless nerve that brings
thoughts of other rooms and years:
dear or darkest happenings:
till the instruments en masse,
all the drums and boisterous brass
blot the sadness out. The fears.

Fortes and fortissimos
toss the vast titanic themes
and a crowd triumphant goes...
and the bells are blazing red
and a city lies ahead
as we dream John Bunyan's dream.

Great gates opening... who are these?
Now, new visions. They become
star-ships from the galaxies
growing larger as we gaze.
People whom we know... a face...

And a heart-beat through the womb.

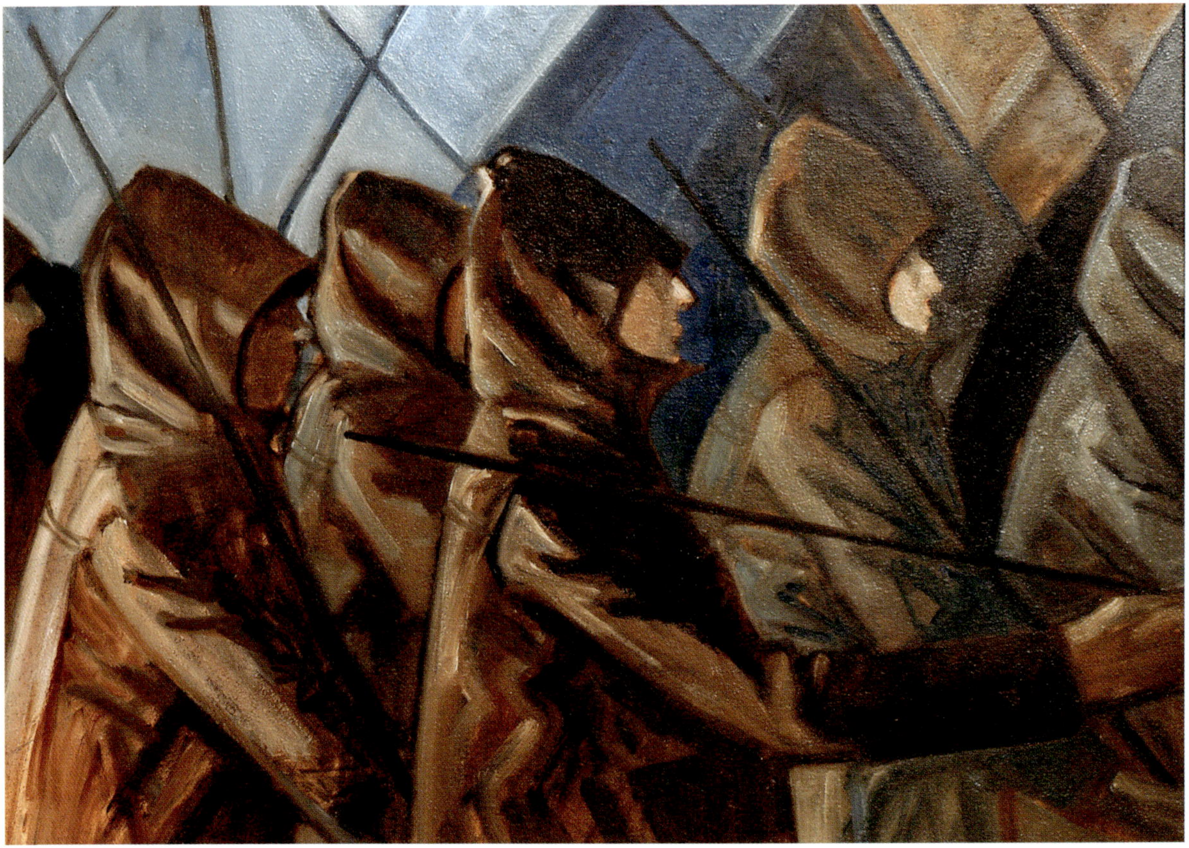

Liberation

When Moses led them forth, the people sang,
And Jewish families even now rejoice
With every hard-won freedom, as it comes.
A teen-age patriot detonates her bombs
Amongst the foreign soldiers, killing two.
She joins them in a common freedom – death.
There comes a time for song, a time to cry.
How can the threadbare words clothe shivering thoughts?
The poet sees a monumental word
Like *Liberation* wearing swords and guns.
But swords are double-edged and guns back-fire.
Old campaign medals bear the deathless words
Like Egypt, Paris, Concord – and the rest.
The poet wonders if his writing hand
Has more compassion than the hand of God
Whose lethal angel flew along the Nile
From Rameses to Thebes and beyond
And opened up the Red Sea like a door
And let it swing right back in Egypt's face.
He sees that topless heroine, Liberty
With tricolor and bayonet and gun
Leading her people through the barricade
Across the quickly liberated dead
With legs and bodies spread – and there a hand
That might that day have moved across a page.
We have no despot kings to trouble us.
We live in peace and breathe a liberal air
And thank our stars or God for food and drink.
But while we feast the starving ghosts go by.

Time for verse

The year has no idea of high or low,
No eyes to look at snowdrops or the sky,
No words to name, no heart to hate or love.

Minutes and hours and days and weeks and years,
The silent movements of the earth and stars,
Will never know how kind or cruel they are.

The heart has no idea of high or low,
No eyes to look at snowdrops or the sky
Only a pump to circulate the blood.

The brain will never think about the heart.
The heart will never grieve about the brain
No more than scattered words will make a verse.

But put them all together, blood and brain
The earth and stars, the snowdrop and the sky,
And all the parts of all the days and years

That make and then unmake us what we are –
Uneasy in a lonely universe,
And doomed to ponder till apocalypse.

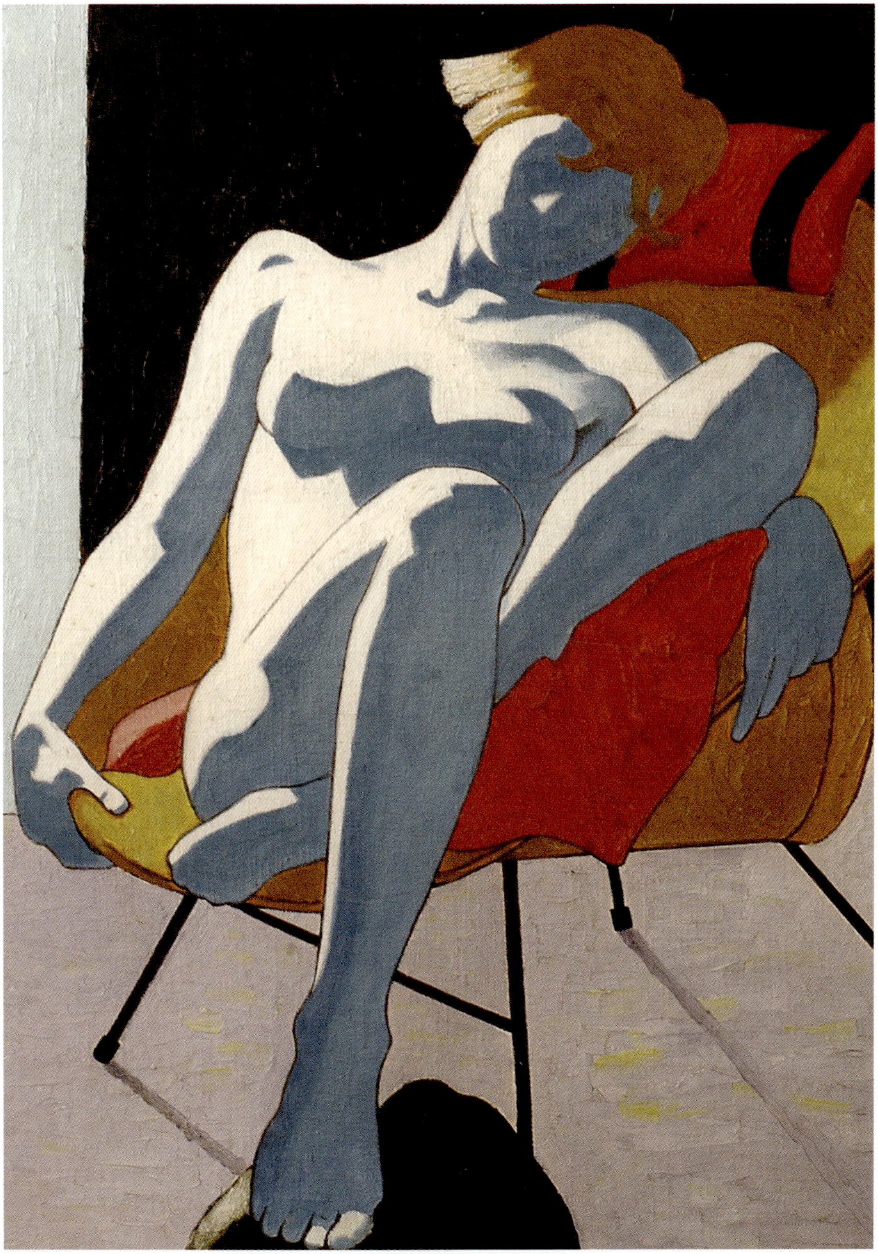

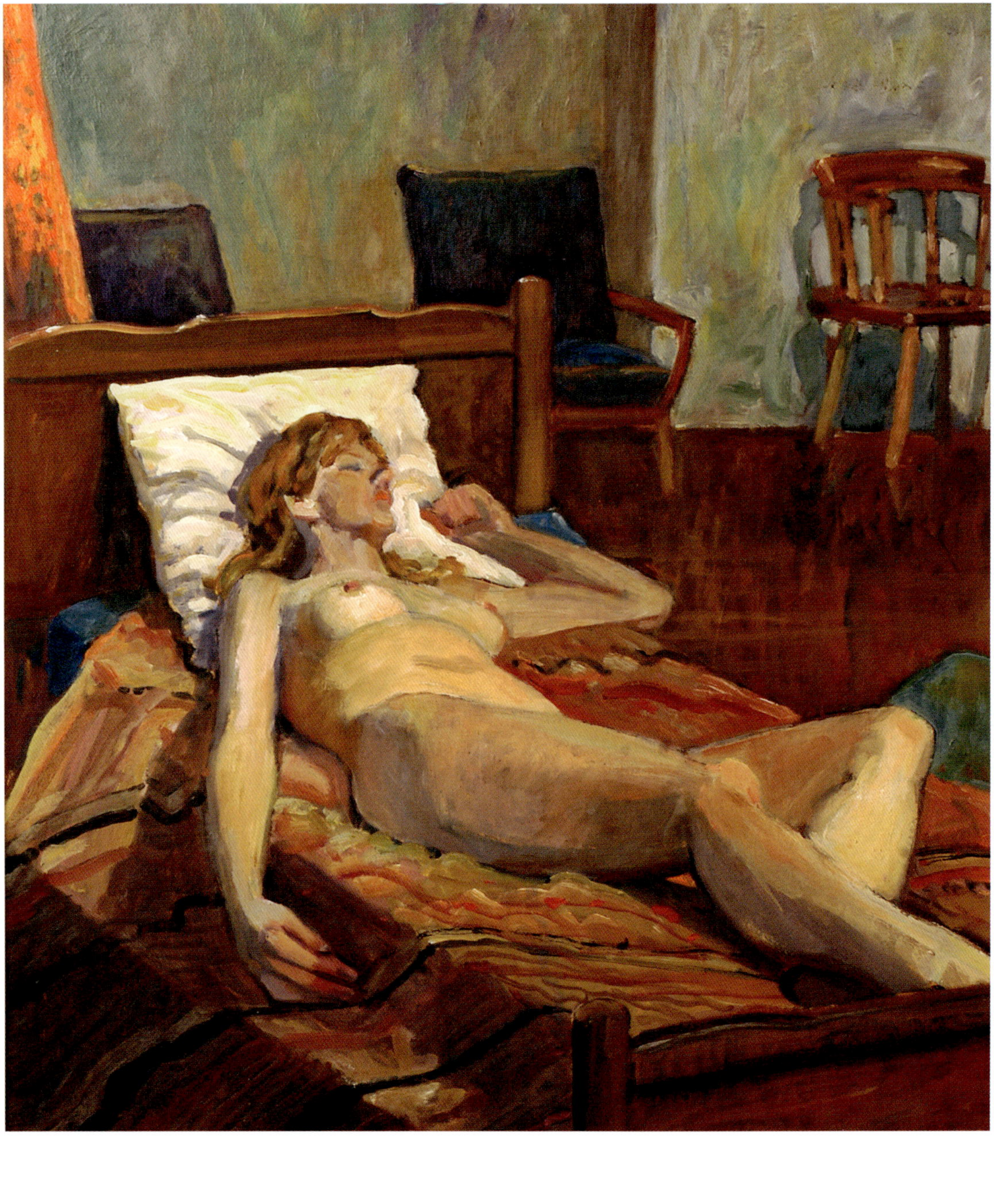

Falling asleep

Each day is spent upon the shores of time,
But nightly, when the tide of sleep pours in,
It takes us, and we sink away below,
Where all the clocks are still.

Down to the place where Morpheus is king,
The Neptune of that vast, resistless sea
Which covers us, and takes us from the shore
Beyond our conscious will.

And then the tide retreats before the dawn,
And casts up sleeping bodies on the shore,
The place of consciousness; the morning time,
And all the clocks are shrill.

A shift of scene

To lie far off, in bed with a foul cough
And a view of elms and roofs and six panes' worth
Of clear sky; here to watch, all the day long,
For a dove, or a black cat, or a puff of smoke
To cause a shift of scene – how could it do so? –
Or to take a pen and write – what else is there
To write but: 'I am not dead, not quite, as yet
Though I lie far off, in bed with a foul cough
And a view of elms and roofs and six panes' worth
Of clear sky'? Tell me, love, are you sick too
And plagued like me with a great hole in the mind
Where all those towers we built, and not on sand,
Have been sucked in and lost: so that it seems
No dove, and no black cat, nor puff of smoke
Can cause a shift of scene and fetch us back
To where we lie as one, in the same bed?

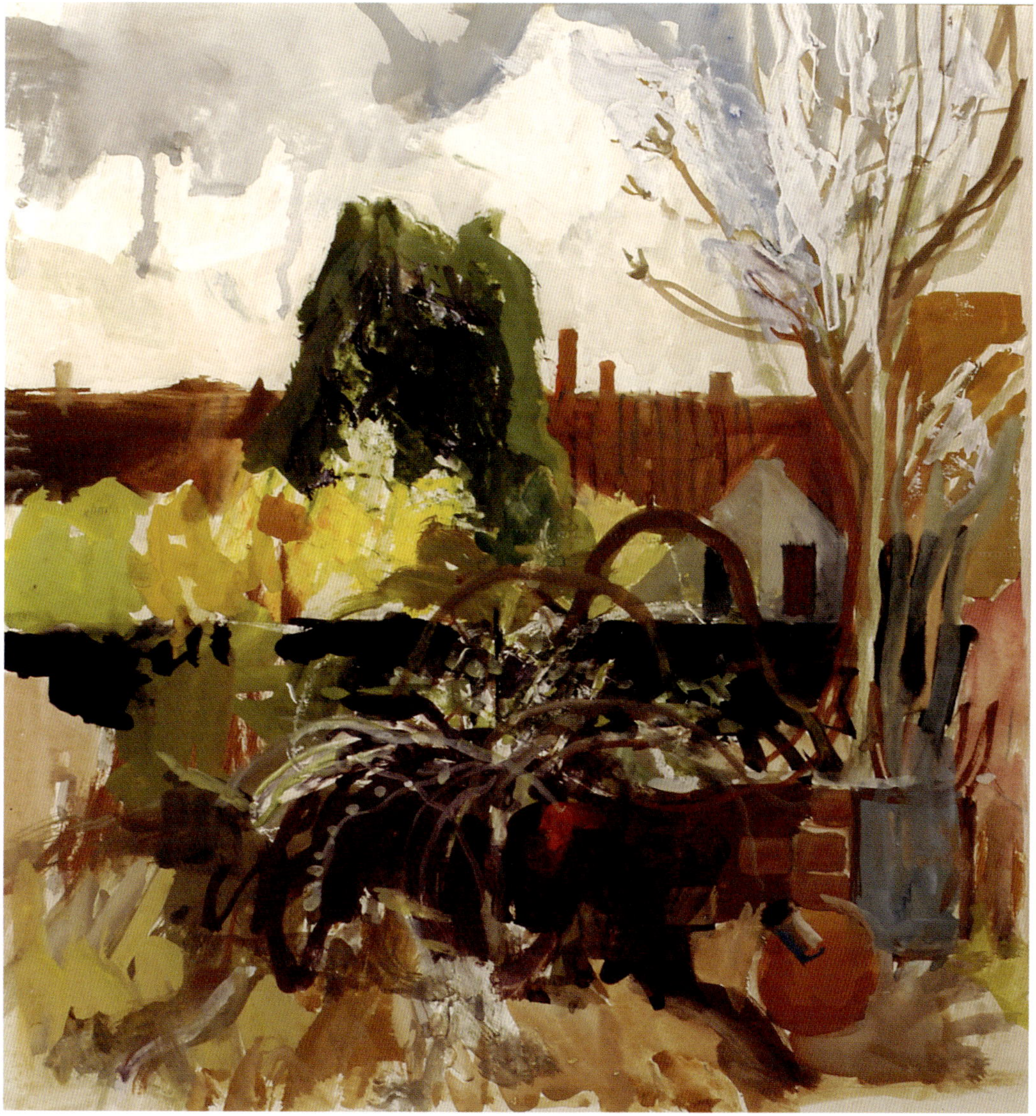

November '89

Not war.
Not the black map slashed
Gashed with spearheads of armies,
But Europe brimming with banners,
Glowing with candles,
Ringing with chants of 'Gorby, Gorby';
Not the tortured towns,
Only the fearful governments falling.
Only the bare bones of trees.
Only the scratching of leaves
Before the wind.
November reddens the embers of old fires
With poppies and pageant,
The quick flick-through of albums,
The black and white, moving on the telly,
The faded voices.
History stirs in her tomb
In a timely month,
Sending a tremor round the hemisphere.
No war. A few sad deaths.
The world looks on.
Berliners bowled along in the strange wind
Wonder what next
And wander west and east
Watching the Wall come down.

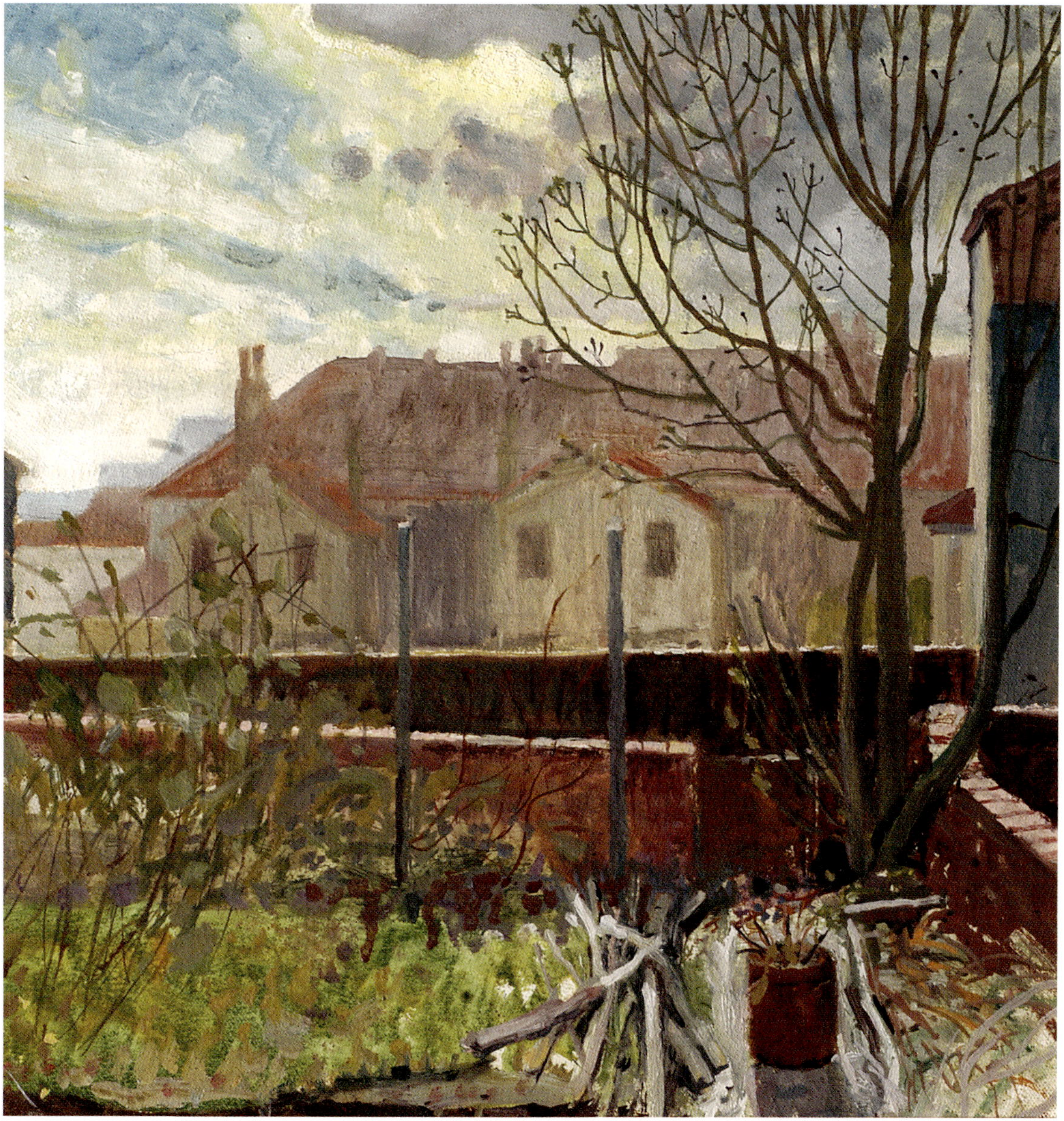

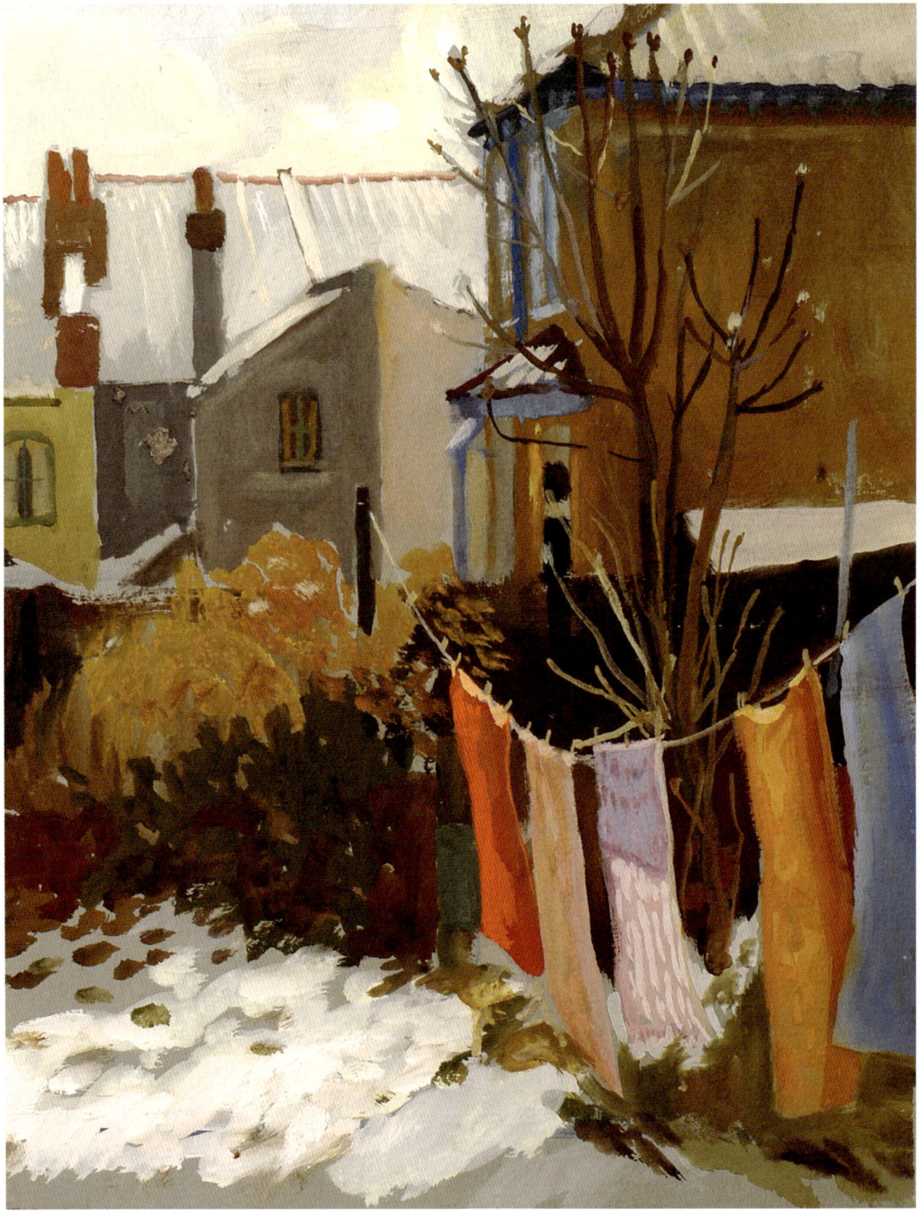

Garden walls in snow

Who needs a colour camera
In the snow?
It's down in black and white,
The statement's plain,
Fir trees, black,
Laden with lumps of snow
And happy as Christmas cards,
Thick white strips along
The garden walls.
Soon a cat will come
With dainty feet
And print a line of spots.
Soon a boy's hands
Will scoop the new snow up.
But this is the pristine picture,
The print untouched.
This is what made
Our bedroom ceilings light,
The
    frozen
        feathers
            falling
Through the night.

A journey

With pagan jubilation men of old
Feasted the turning of their god, the Sun,
Towards the wintry forests of the north.
With greater gladness Eastern travellers told
A jealous king, 'We seek another one –
Not Herod, but a King of all the Earth'.
At least, as Eliot says: 'There was a birth'.
'There was a birth'. Is there a birth today
Of hope, despite the contraceptive power
Of ancient fear? Will Wise Men journey forth
With golden gifts of precious food to lay
At tiny feet, even at this late hour?
That Holy Child was meant to show the worth
Of every helpless, undernourished birth.

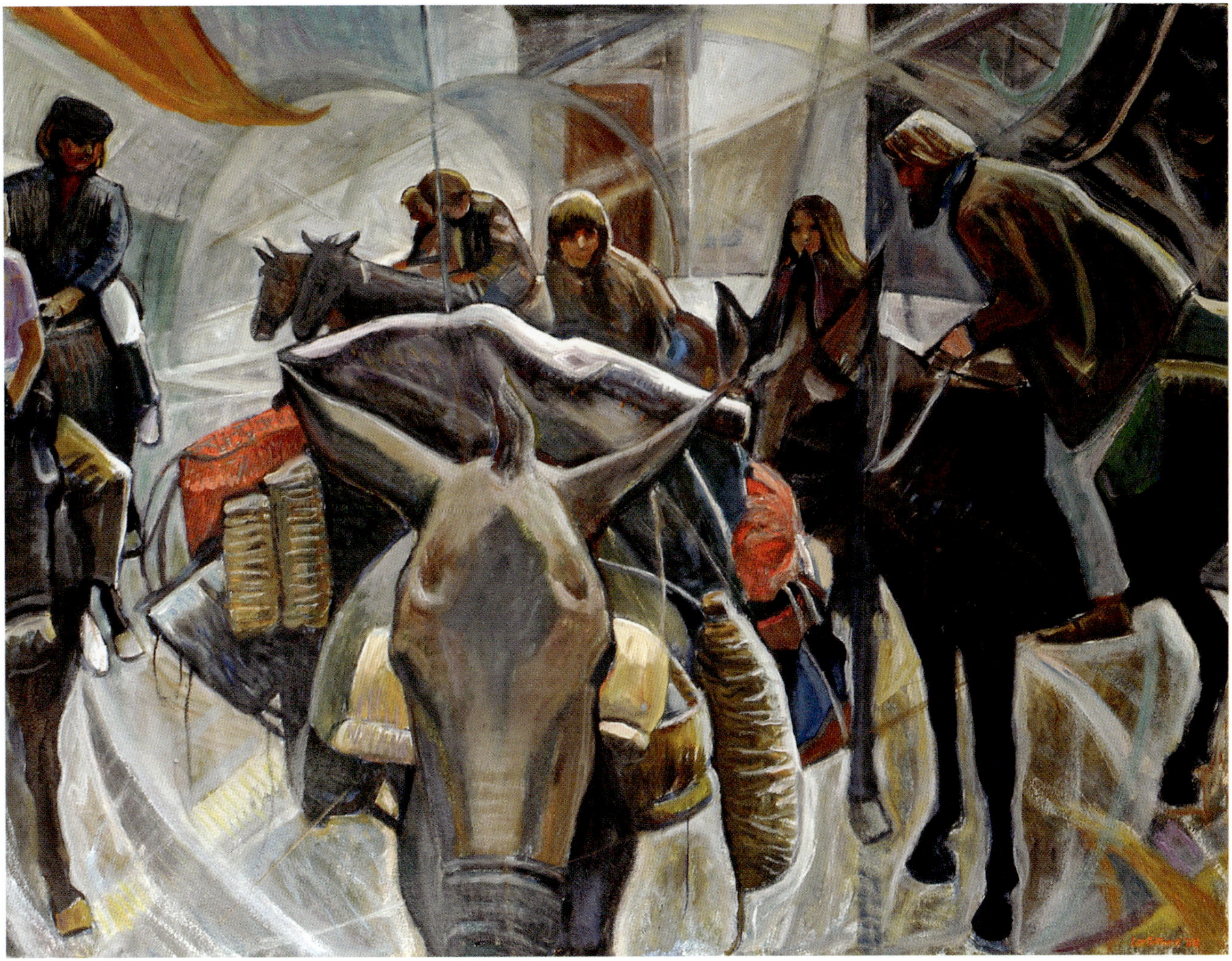

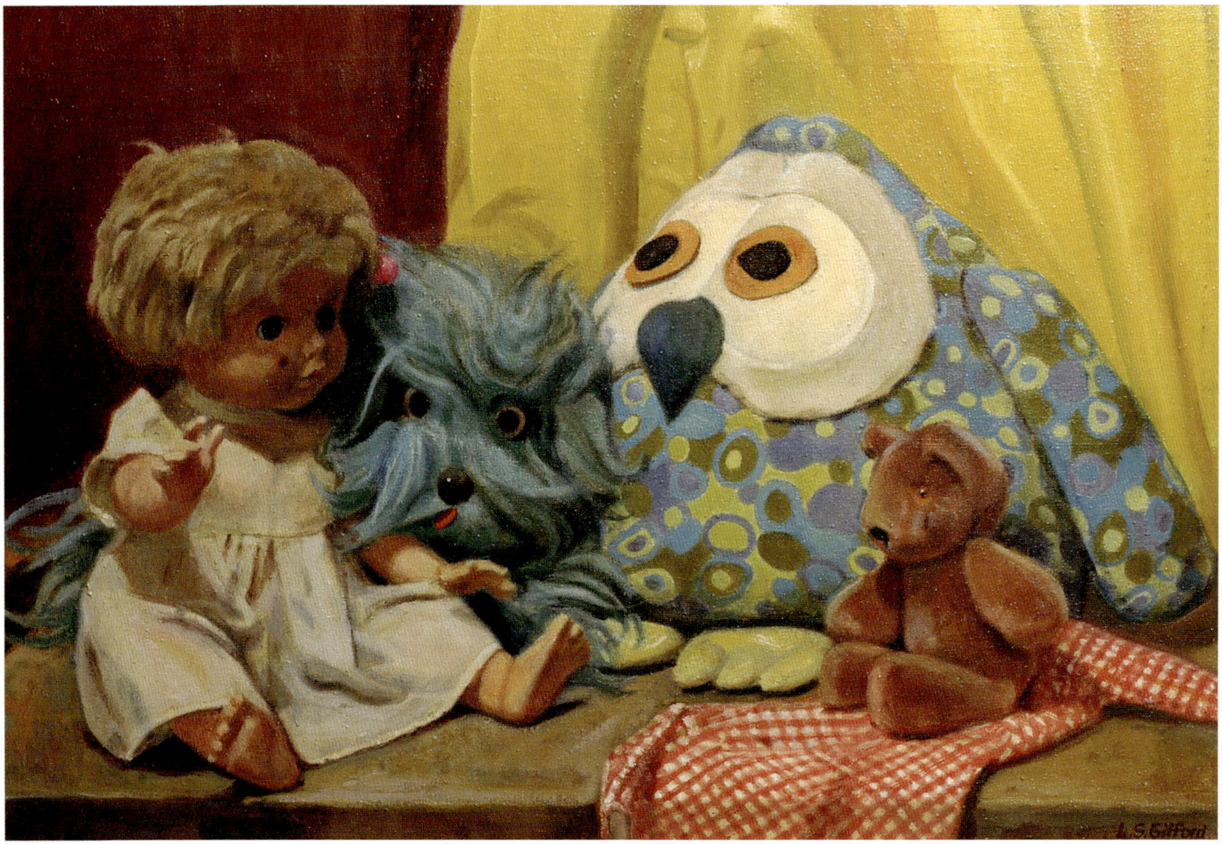
L. S. Gifford

Christmas Day

Christmas again! It's all wrapping, wrapping!
God in emergency, bandaged and swaddled.

This winter morning is wrapped all in silence,
and families in the familiar.
But by St. Paul's peace women go wrapped up
as if against the nuclear winter.

Clamorous children tear the morning space
and sleep from their parents
as furiously they flay the stubborn parcels.
Under the clutter and clatter of paper
somebody says: 'It's just what I wanted' –
politely or grateful.
Now we can wrap flesh and bone round the table,
chocolates or chicken, forgetful of waistlines.
Later or sooner a tentative finger
Switches the telly on. Now we can goggle at
all kinds of horror, but wrapped up in fiction
with greetings from Agatha Christmas
and Dickens.

Christmas is past, and all the unwrapping.
Did we unwrap something new, something given –
Peace and new treasure and satisfied hunger?
Bethlehem's child was not merely for children.

January poem

The sad sky clears, and the south wind
that drove the spears of rain
ruffles the winter leaves
and splinters the surface of pools.

Morning shoppers, wrapped in warm clothes,
hugging their secret thoughts,
are tugged and plucked at
by the puckish wind.

Then, for a second, you see it,
the genuine glory, the real
poem just waiting for words
that slip away helplessly fading.

Like a ghost it slips
away from the words you are left with –
all you have now to record
the sudden heart-warming.

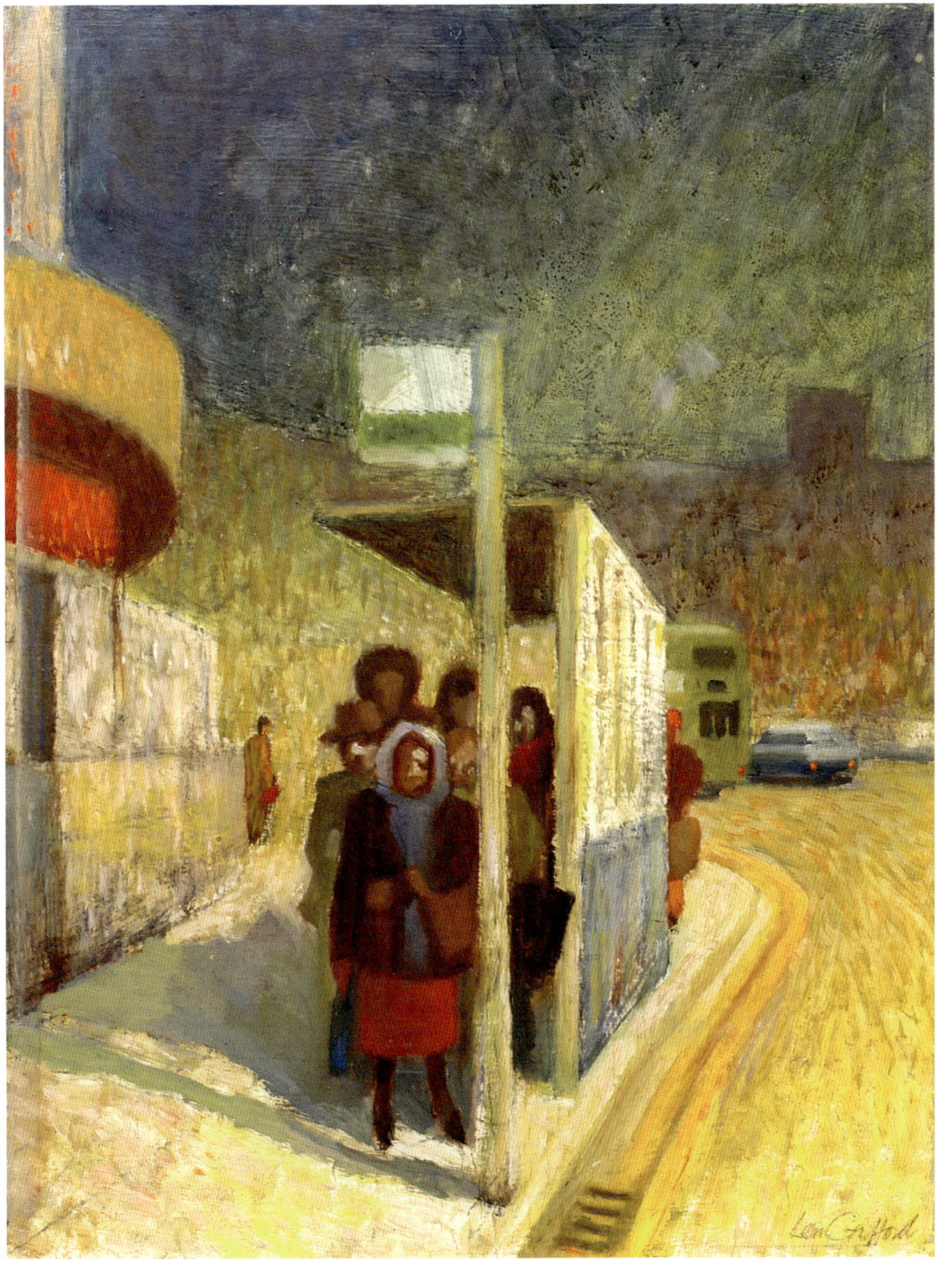

Storm

His name is Storm, Amphibious, massive winged
Inhabitant of oceans and of skies,
His monstrous body, tiger-like, is ringed
With isobars. His savage blackened teeth
Advance like pressure fronts of cold and ice
Or heat and steam. And back and forth beneath
The seas or where he makes the thunder roll
He goes. His habitat, his native heath,
Is fixed between Equator and the Pole.
Storm is his name. And lest he should attack
We cringe and cower behind our harbour wall,
Or pray for life when caught upon his back.
But though his battering claw brings bloody death,
Beneath this awful guise he's life and breath.

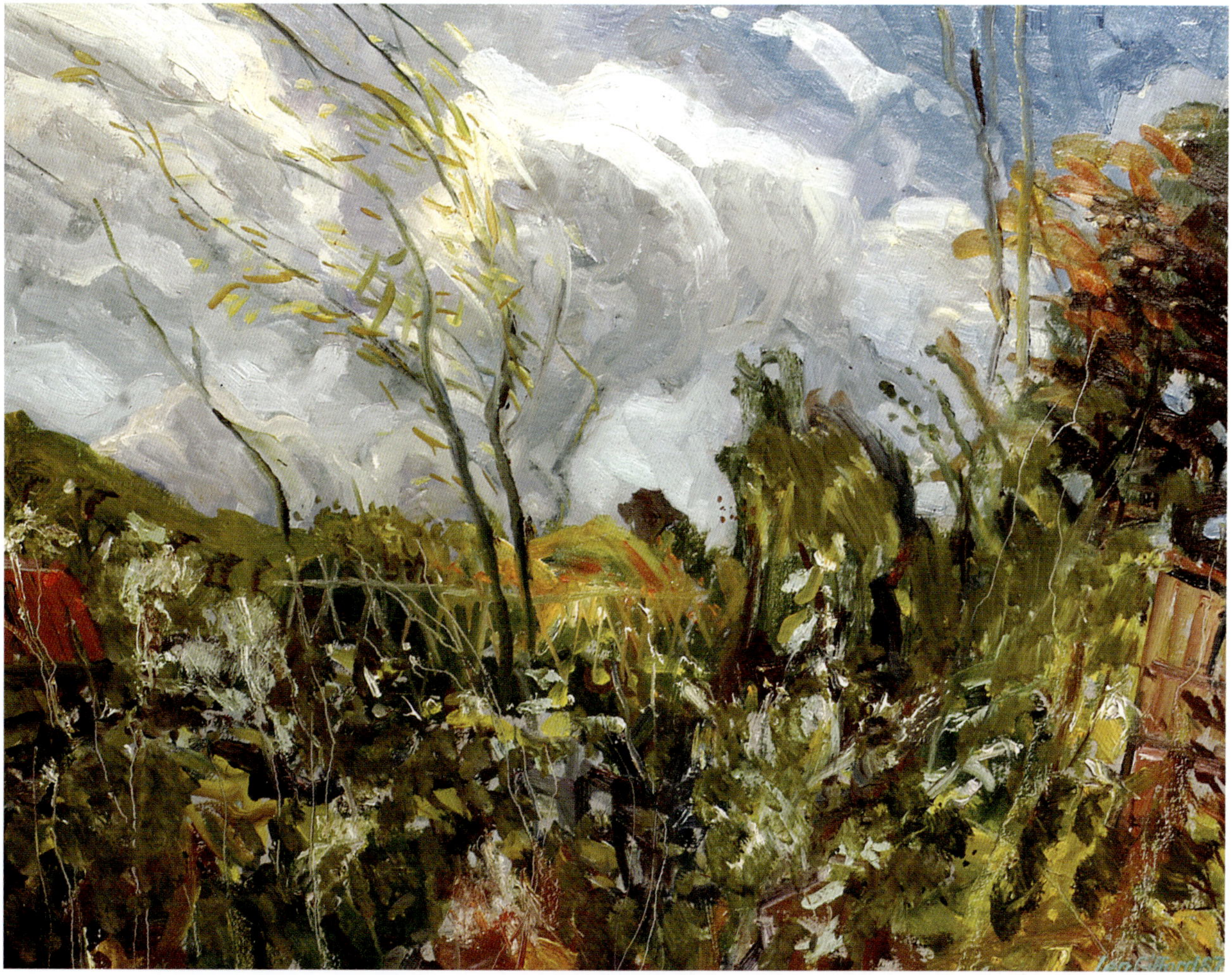

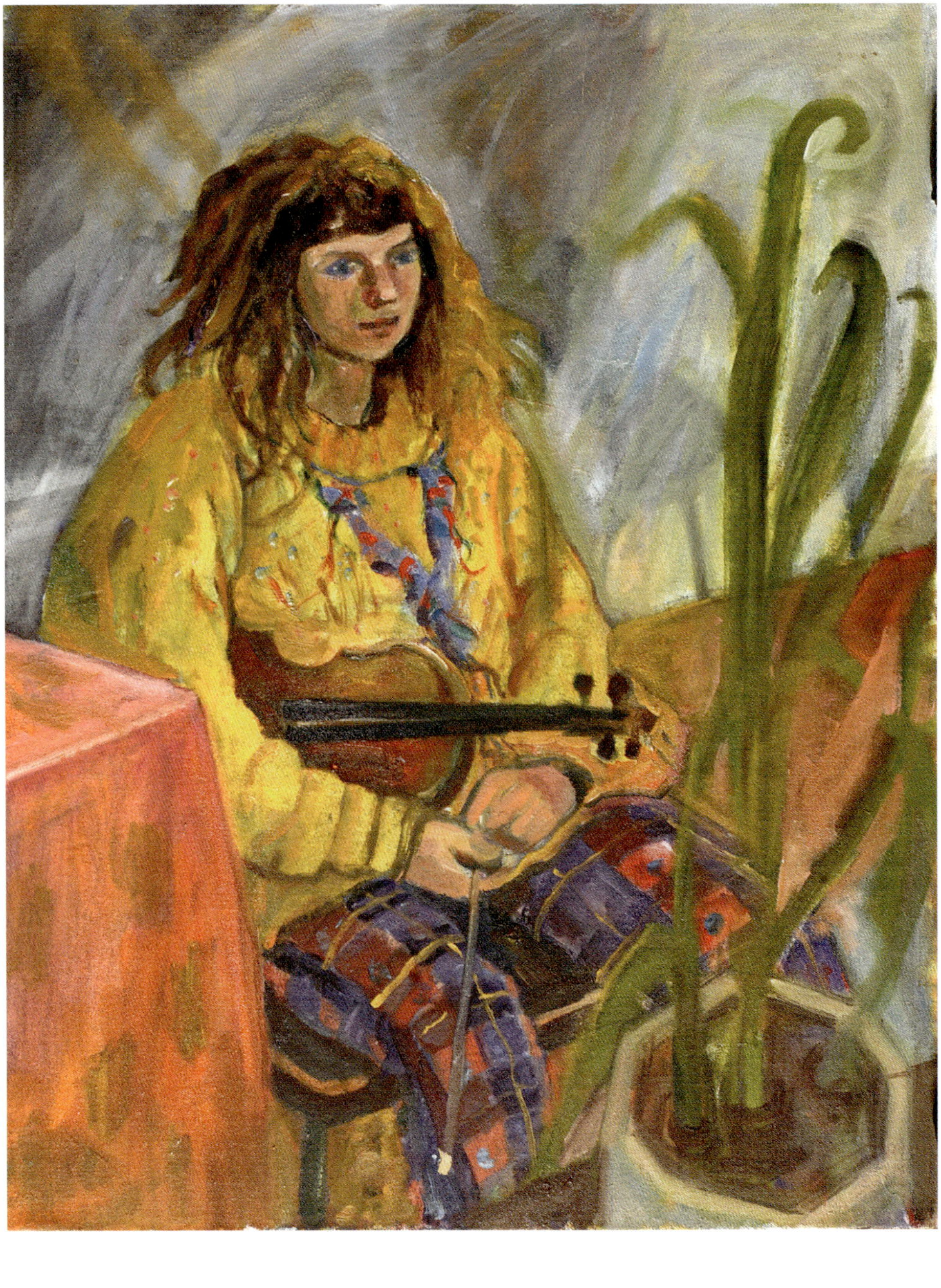

Anniversary of Beethoven (any musical figure)

In days of ardent music-loving youth,
We'd sit behind the stage, our usual place.
(The seats were cheaper then, to tell the truth)
And we could watch Sir Thomas Beecham's face.

Not when he turned to speak, with earthy jest,
But when he strove to bring all Heaven down
About our ravished ears. At his behest
The strings and woodwinds sang with glorious sound

And magic Mozart lived. The baton's wave
Transformed the old familiar overture.
Like Mendelssohn *we* stood near Fingal's Cave
And saw the breakers crashing on the shore.

And is Sir Thomas now among his peers,
With Delius perhaps, new blessed with sight,
Talking to mighty Beethoven, who hears,
Delivered from his cruel mortal plight?

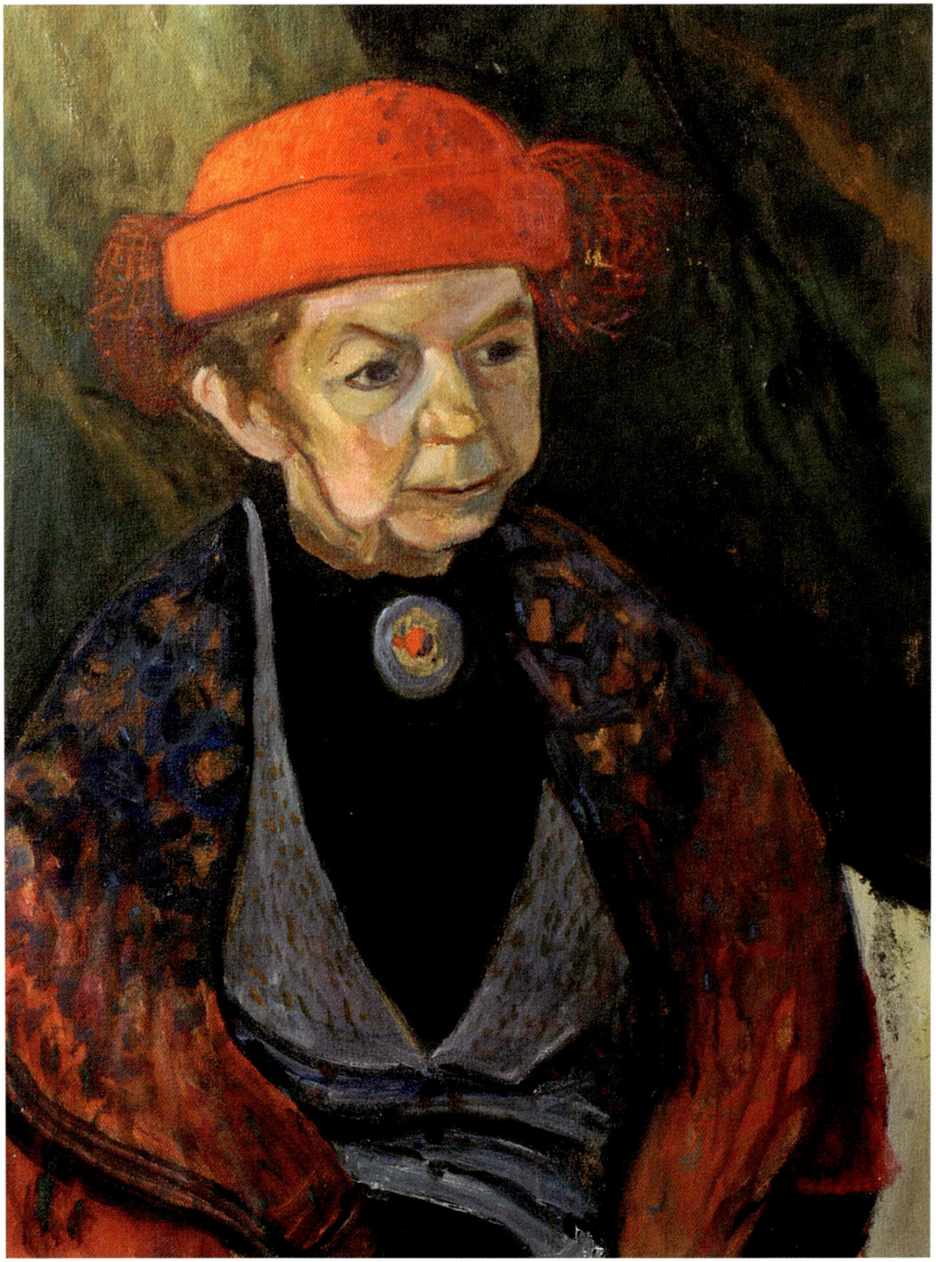

Mournful numbers

O what a piece of work is man –
a creature who, with any luck
may breathe five hundred million times
and sleep for twenty years.

How many dreams and hopes and fears,
hot dinners, hair-cuts, cups of tea
and toothpaste tubes and rainy days,
how many miles on the clock
and scribbled sheets of poetry
and acts of love and aspirins
and library books and shoes and bills?

How many things you might have done
three hundred million breaths ago
that, with an older pair of lungs
you won't do now?

How much arithmetic remains
before five thousand million cells
of blood break down for ever?
No-one knows.